EGYPT

By the staff of Editions Berlitz

Preface

A new kind of travel guide for the jet age—Berlitz has packed all you need to know about Egypt into this compact and colourful book, one of an extensive series on the world's top tourist areas.

Like our phrase books and dictionaries, this book fits your pocket—in both size and price. It also aims to fit your travel needs:

- It combines easy reading with fast facts: what to see and do, where to shop, what to eat.

- An authoritative A-to-Z "blueprint" fills the back of the book, giving clear-cut answers to all your questions, from "What time do the banks open?" to "Is the water safe to drink?"—plus how to get there, when to go and what to budget.

- Easy-to-read maps in full colour pinpoint the sights you'll want to see in Cairo as well as in Alexandria and Upper Egypt.

In short, this handy guide will help you enjoy your trip to Egypt. From the ancient Pyramids of Giza to the bustling bazaars of modern Cairo, from the mysteries of the Valley of the Kings to the beaches of Alexandria, Berlitz tells you clearly and concisely what it's all about.

How to use this guide
If time is short, look for items to visit which are printed in bold type in this book, e.g. **Coptic Museum.** Those sights most highly recommended are not only given in bold type but also carry our traveller symbol, e.g. **Tutankhamon's treasure.**

Area specialist: Tom Brosnahan
Photography: Luc Chessex
Illustrations: Aude Aquoise
We are particularly grateful to Jean O'Hanlon for her help in the preparation of this book. We should also like to thank EgyptAir and Assem Tawfik as well as Mounira Fouad and Abdel Rahman of the Egyptian Tourist Office in Geneva for their valuable assistance.

4   Cartography: Falk-Verlag, Hamburg.

Contents

Maps: Nile Valley p. 11, Central Cairo pp. 26–27, Alexandria pp. 48–49, Upper Egypt p. 55.
Cover: Pyramids and Sphinx of Giza.

Egypt and the Egyptians

Vast expanses of burning Saharan wasteland, the limitless sands broken only by dusty caravan tracks: how could such terrain have given birth 5,000 years ago to one of man's most awe-inspiring civilizations? Almost every Egyptian mystery has the same solution: the Nile. Gathering waters from deep in Africa, the mighty river makes its way through the desert to the Mediterranean Sea. Without the Nile, there would be no Egypt.

To understand the importance of the river for Egyptians, stand on its western bank at Aswan. Here, the desert reaches so close to the water that you can pick up a handful of sand and throw it in. For more than 600 miles—from Abu Simbel to Cairo—narrow fields full of irrigated crops line the banks. The cloudless sky adds its blessing, the hot sun nurturing no fewer than three harvests a year. The early Egyptians saw divinity in the sun which returned faithfully every day: they

Egyptian extremes: slow caravans in vast deserts, and fast-moving Cairene buses always packed full.

named it Ra, and raised great temples in its honour.

What happened to these ancient Egyptians? Believe it or not, their descendants still live along the Nile. They accepted Christianity as taught them by Saint Mark, and founded one of Christendom's oldest churches. Called Copts, they still play a significant role in their country's affairs, and Coptic churches can be found in almost all Egyptian towns.

Between 1100 and 332 B.C. came Libyans, Persians and black Africans from Nubia. Then, around the 7th century, Arabs started to pour into Egypt's rich delta adding their own languages and customs which still thrive today.

Egypt has always held an irresistible fascination for tourists and it's not difficult to understand why. Pyramids, palms, the Nile, the desert, the Sphinx—all these are enough to make any traveller dream of at least one trip to Egypt in a lifetime. But scratch the surface of a pyramid and you'll find Egypt's true glory, for this is a land whose history and ancient civilization are of inestimable value to archaeologists and anthropologists, theologians and philosophers, art historians and other scholars from almost every field of culture and learning.

And it is this deeply rooted sense of history, which even a jet-age tourist senses, that makes the country unique. As you visit the four mighty stone figures of Ramesis II in Abu Simbel, it's impossible not to feel a certain awe about a civilization which gave a pharaoh the status of a god. Tramping through the sacred temples of Luxor and Karnak and the eerie city of the dead at Thebes will make you realize how serious these ancient Egyptians were about their religion. Elsewhere, you'll constantly see the sights and hear the names that make up the colourful mosaic of Egyptian life: Memphis, Horus, Tutankhamon, Antony and Cleopatra, El-Alamein, Alexandria, the Suez Canal. But just as the Rosetta Stone provided the clue to understanding ancient hieroglyphs, the key to the heart of modern Egypt is, undeniably, Cairo.

Compared to the eternal life of the river, Cairo is a "new" city—only 1,000 years old. In the shadow of Giza's pyramids, Cairenes have raised countless monuments to the glory of Islam and made their city the cultural capital of Arabic civiliza-

Ramesis II repeats himself at awe-inspiring Abu Simbel temple.

8

tion. Throughout the world, Moslems still look to Cairo as the treasure-house of Islamic art, architecture and learning.

As capital of the most populous Arab nation on earth, Cairo confronts urgent problems. Its population grows at the incredible rate of 3,300 persons a day; even crumbling medieval tombs have been converted to dwellings in an effort to house them all. The city's streets are thronged with armies of pedestrians and legions of cars, all stirring up the blanket of fine

Teeming Tahrir Square, symbol of Egypt's progress—and problems.

desert dust which infrequent and brief rains can never wash away. Noise is a constant bother. Public services are so over-taxed that buses run with passengers on the fenders and hanging out of the windows.

With all its excess population, Cairo is not the land of do-it-yourself, but of have-someone-do-it-for-you. From carrying your luggage to fetching a newspaper, you'll get more help than you need for a small tip.

But despite difficult problems, Egyptians are eternally hopeful. Every day the newspapers announce another momentous new project designed to catapult the country into the 21st century. The plans may get bogged down in skeins of red tape, but one can't give up hope. After all, the Aswan High Dam performed modern miracles, controlling the annual flooding of the Nile which had occurred since the beginning of time, and providing enough electricity for the entire country's needs. In any case, it doesn't help to worry.

Long-suffering Cairenes draw confidence from their city's triumphant past and their country's glorious history: Egypt is eternal, the Nile's not going to stop flowing. As for the inconveniences of city life, *ma'alish!* Never mind!

A Brief History

Years, even centuries, lose meaning as one leaps back in time to the misty ages of 3000 B.C.* Before this date, Egyptian life is shrouded in mystery, though we know that the inhabitants were an artistically gifted and vigorous people. They already had a sophisticated hieroglyphic symbol system, and when they invented papyrus by pounding strips of Nile grass together the written history of ancient Egypt began to unfold.

Old and Middle Kingdoms

King Menes (1st Dynasty, 3000 B.C.) united Upper and Lower Egypt, and was the first to wear the "double crown" so often seen in pharaonic art. The capital was at Memphis, a short distance south of Cairo. Unity brought Egypt wealth, power and progress, and some three centuries later the Old Kingdom (2780–2250 B.C.) headed by King Zoser of the 3rd Dynasty was established. He built the step pyramid of Saqqara, inaugurating the era of the great pyramids. Within 200 years mathematics and man-

power organization had advanced so far that Cheops and his son Chephren were able to construct the colossal pyramids and sphinx at Giza. Crowning this astounding human achievement with the halo of divinity, pharaohs of the 5th Dynasty (2440–2315 B.C.) proclaimed themselves to be sons of the great sun god Ra. But saying one is a god and being a god are different matters, and as time wore on royal authority declined. The Old Kingdom

---

* All dates given before the birth of Christ must be regarded as approximate.

was brought to an end by civil war around 2250 B.C.

The Middle Kingdom lasted over four centuries (2000–1570 B.C.) during which time Egypt re-established itself as a rich and strong nation. Pharaohs stood at the top of a feudal order, and powerful nobles controlled each of the *nomes* (provinces) of the kingdom. Supported by his vassals, the king marched at the head of his army from the new capital at Thebes (Luxor) south to Nubia and east

King Zoser's Step Pyramid set off the pyramid-building craze.

into Palestine, conquering all in his path. Foreign adventures could be afforded because of the immense new wealth brought by significant advances in irrigation, especially in the desert province of Fayyoum.

As the conquerors' fortunes increased, their lands became more and more desirable to Egypt's warlike neighbours. **13**

One enemy people, the Hyksos, had a secret weapon to overcome even the bravest and most determined Egyptian footsoldier: the horse chariot. When in the 17th century B.C. they rolled swiftly across Sinai and into the fertile delta, the pharaohs were forced to retreat to Thebes (Luxor). Triumphantly the Hyksos chiselled signs of their victories on the walls of tombs and temples, where figures of horses and

---

Historical Key

Egyptian history is so long it soon becomes bewildering. (By the time you've mastered it all, you'll be ready for a Ph.D.) Here's a simplified key to the major periods:

Old Kingdom	3000–2250 B.C.	1st to 6th Dynasties; pyramids at Giza and Saqqara
Middle Kingdom	2000–1570 B.C.	11th and 12th Dynasties; Hyksos chariot invasion
New Kingdom	1570–1100 B.C.	18th to 20th Dynasties; tombs and temples at Luxor, Abu Simbel
Libyan, Nubian, Assyrian, Persian Invasions	1100–332 B.C.	21st to 30th Dynasties; decline and civil strife
Ptolemaic Period	332–30 B.C.	Ptolemies I to XIV; Alexander the Great's successors
Roman-Byzantine Period	30 B.C.–A.D. 639	Saint Mark brings Christianity about A.D. 40
Arab Empire	639–1251	Umayyad, Abbasid, Fatimid, Ayyubid Dynasties
Mameluke Dynasties	1251–1517	Cairo mosques and mausoleums
Ottoman Turkish Period	1517–1914	Mohammed Ali gains control, 1811; Suez Canal opens, 1869
Kingdom of Egypt	1914–1952	Mohammed Ali Dynasty; British control
Republican Period	Begins 1953	Aswan High Dam completed, 1972

wheeled vehicles remain to this day. For a century the Hyksos ruled Lower Egypt, but their unassailable power stopped where the chariots could go no farther, at the southern tip of the flat and easily crossed delta.

New Kingdom

The threat from the Hyksos had forced the pharaohs to think over the way the country was run, and after their expulsion in 1570 B.C. a number of reforms were undertaken. First, the rulers succeeded in taking away the power of the great feudal nobles and concentrating it all in their own hands. Then they built chariots thus improving their military capacity, and soon Egypt became an imperial state, well-organized, disciplined and headed by a monarch greedy for foreign conquests and personal glory. During the New Kingdom (1570–1100 B.C.) ancient Egypt reached the pinnacle of its splendour. The massive temples and tombs at Luxor, Karnak and Abu Simbel were built, and Egyptian armies brought back rich booty and hundreds of slaves from Syria and deep in Africa. The wealth of the country was unparalleled, and much of it went to glorify the god-kings who ruled it.

Some of Egypt's greatest rulers were those of the 18th Dynasty. The three pharaohs named Thutmose vastly extended the empire's borders. Hatshepsut, wife of Thutmose II and stepmother of Thutmose III, ruled for a time as queen of Egypt, and built herself a fabulous funerary temple at Deir el-Bahari. Amenophis III (1417–1379 B.C.) reigned when New Kingdom Egypt was at its glittering zenith. He made large contributions to the building of the Great Temple of Amon at Karnak as well as two gigantic seated figures called the Colossi of Memnon, fashioned in his own image. His son Amenophis IV ignored statecraft and warfare to concentrate on mystical matters, and decreed a new religion: the age-old pantheon of Egyptian gods was to be displaced by the One True God, Aton, whose symbol was a simple solar disc with beneficent rays extending to earth. Amenophis changed his own name to Akhenaton ("He Who Pleases Aton"), and with Queen Nefertiti moved his capital to the place now called Tell El-Amarna in Middle Egypt. But he made bitter enemies of the powerful priests of Amon at Thebes. When he died, the country was in disarray and his young son-in-law Tutankhaton

(1361–1351 B.C.—who later changed his name to Tutankhamon) had such a short reign that it was impossible to restore order.

The 18th Dynasty ended as power was usurped by an energetic and able soldier, Ramesis I, founder of the 19th Dynasty. His successor, Seti, won back all of Egypt's foreign possessions by renewed conquests. Then came Ramesis II. This pharaoh had some trouble maintaining the empire, but none in becoming the greatest and most prolific builder Egypt had ever known. His long reign (1304–1237 B.C.) saw the huge temple rise at Abu Simbel, and the great hypostyle hall finished at Karnak, plus countless other gigantic monuments, usually containing a generous ration of statues in his own image. With a firm hand Ramesis II subdued the Semitic tribes which had been a cause of disorder in his eastern provinces. One tribe, the Israelites, he kept under strict control for years before allowing them to leave captivity in Egypt and return to the land of their forefathers.

Pharaohs of the 20th Dynasty preserved Egypt's greatness until 1100 B.C. After that, although later dynasties struggled to return to past glory, none could regain it. Foreign invasions became frequent, and by 332 B.C. the last Egyptian pharaoh had fallen from the throne forever. Alexander the Great conquered the country with little resistance, and pharaonic Egypt's fabled life was at an end.

Under Greece and Rome

When Alexander died and his vast empire crumbled in 323 B.C., his generals seized control of the fragments. The governor of Egypt, Ptolemy, assumed the title of pharaoh in 305 but the country was divided into two cultures now, and the Hellenistic dominated the Egyptian. Alexandria, the conqueror's city on the Mediterranean shore, was the most civilized and important in the Hellenistic world. But the power of learning and the excellent library which were Alexandria's glory could do little against the legions of Rome.

For twenty years (51–30 B.C.) Queen Cleopatra VII used wit and charm first on Caesar, then on the Roman general Mark Antony, to keep her country free (see box). But Caesar's heir Octavius (later Augustus) was immune to her fascination and set out to take control of Egypt. When Mark Antony was defeated at the naval battle of Actium (30 B.C.) the queen committed suicide,

Cleopatra

Lots of Ptolemaic princesses were given the name Cleopatra, but it was Cleopatra VII (69–30 B.C.) who left her mark on history. Married to her younger brother Ptolemy XII when she was seventeen years old, she later overthrew him with Caesar's aid. She followed the conqueror to Rome, deserted her second husband—another brother—and eventually bore a son, whom she named Caesarion. (It has never been unquestionably established that Caesarion's true father was Julius Caesar, but it suited everybody to believe it at the time.) For a while Caesarion co-reigned with his mother as Ptolemy XIV.

Sometime after Caesar's murder, Mark Antony showed up in Egypt and also fell quickly and completely under Cleopatra's bewitching spell. They were married in 36 B.C. At the end of her reign, after the crushing naval defeat at Actium, she had a servant bring her a basket of figs, containing a serpent. She bit a fig and the snake bit her.

Despite the evident charms she seems to have had for Julius Caesar and Mark Antony, historians record that Cleopatra was neither strikingly beautiful, nor popular with the Romans, who either feared or despised her.

and Hellenistic Egypt died with her. For centuries to come the land would be only a distant province of the Roman Empire, ruled first from Rome and later from Constantinople.

The Arab Empire

The wave of conquering armies which poured forth from Arabia in the 7th century is one of the most baffling phenomena in history. Before the Prophet Mohammed's time, the Arabs consisted of only a few dozen Semitic tribes living in a hot and dusty land. To earn their dates and camel's milk, they traded by camel caravan or carried out raids on their neighbours. But with the coming of Islam ("Submission to God's Will"), the Arabs set out on conquests which were to change the world.

Mohammed, a merchant in the city of Mecca, was a pensive sort who would go off to a cool cave in the mountains to think and ponder. During one such retreat in A.D. 612 he heard a celestial voice commanding him to write and communicate his vision. During the next twenty years, until his death in 632, Mohammed produced the 114 *suras* (verses) which make up the Koran, the beautiful work which became the poetry, law and inspiration of the Arabic people.

In the early years of Islam, believers were organized into a small, close-knit society headed by Mohammed himself. As the community expanded, armies were formed, and military operations begun. Within a century of Mohammed's death, Arab forces had conquered all the Middle East including Persia, all of North Africa, and even parts of Spain and France.

Egypt was among the first countries to fall, invaded by the Arabs in 639. They made their military camp of El-Fustat, the country's capital. Within 300 years Egypt had become one of the Arab empire's most important political, military and religious centres. Then, in about 968, a powerful dynasty called the Fatimids swept in from the Maghreb to seize Egypt and establish a new capital, Misr Al-Qahira, the City of Mars. Despite the decadence that was later to set in, Fatimid rule was vigorous at first and Cairo lived one of its richest cultural periods during the two centuries of their domination. The renowned mosque and university of El-Azhar date from these times and still remain a spiritual beacon to all Islam, the buildings recalling the highest glory of Fatimid architecture.

The empire of the Fatimids was overrun by the armies of Saladin in 1169. Saladin, famous for his campaigns against the Crusaders in Palestine and Syria, established his own dynasty in Egypt, the Ayyubids. His descendants were ousted by a new wave of usurpers, mostly Turkish soldiers who had been slaves (mameluke) of the Ayyubids. In a series of short and violent reigns, Mameluke strongmen succeeded one another from 1251 to 1517. Despite the instability of their rule, Mameluke might spread through Syria and Palestine. In Cairo, they built countless palaces and mosques of exquisite beauty.

Mameluke power was defeated, but not destroyed, when Egypt was conquered by the fast-moving and efficient armies of the Ottoman Turks in 1517. Three years later, Suleiman the Magnificent came to the throne in Constantinople (Istanbul), ushering in the Ottoman Empire's most brilliant and powerful era. But it didn't last long and when he died his dominions began a period of decline lasting some three and half centuries. The Egyptian province lost the benefits of

El-Azhar, glory of Islamic Cairo, is the Oxford of the Moslem world.

efficient government and internal order as provincial Mameluke lords clamoured for many of their old prerogatives from the Ottoman pasha in Cairo. Instability returned with the Mameluke rulers and Egypt lived from crisis to crisis in a decadent and backward culture.

Napoleon and Mohammed Ali

The modern world first came into contact with Egypt when a French military expedition headed by a young officer named Napoleon Bonaparte reached Alexandria in 1798. Though their primary interest was to block England's Red Sea route to India, the expedition included a group of scientists and archaeologists. Napoleon's efforts brought a certain order and discipline to Egypt's government for a short time, and laid the foundation for later archaeological expeditions. In the momentous battle of Abukir (1798), the English crushed the French forces who three years later were to sail for home. Egypt seemed ready to slip into torpor and anarchy again.

France's Princess Eugenie, Austria's Franz-Josef, Egypt's Ismail in glittering array as Suez opens.

Among the Ottoman troops who had arrived to counter the French invasion was a young officer called Mohammed Ali. With considerable cunning and force, he succeeded in seizing power and having himself appointed Pasha of Egypt by the sultan. Then on May 1, 1811, he invited all his rivals, the Mameluke notables, to a banquet in the Citadel at Cairo. As each Mameluke entered the thick stone walls, the gates were slammed shut behind him and the new pasha's troops quietly removed his head from his body. Mameluke political power, an important factor in Egypt since 1251, ended for good that night.

Fascinated by glimpses of modern methods he had seen in Napoleon's army, Mohammed Ali proceeded to reform his own and to build a fleet on Western lines, using European advisors. Moves were made to modernize agriculture and commerce, and cotton was planted in newly irrigated lands. The country started to produce great wealth, and though the people remained desperately poor, the ruler was fabulously rich and powerful. Between 1832 and 1841 Mohammed Ali waged war on his sovereign in Istanbul twice and almost succeeded in capturing the Ottoman capital. Forced to recognize the virtually independent power of his onetime vassal, the sultan decreed that the office of Pasha of Egypt should be hereditary in the house of Mohammed Ali. Later this title of *pasha* was upgraded to *khedive*, just short of "king".

But later rulers of the House of Mohammed Ali could not live up to their ancestor's energy and vision. Khedive Ismail, who ruled from 1863 to 1879, championed the plan for a Suez Canal, but his ambitious undertakings were financed by unscrupulous bankers. When the khedive could not repay the millions in gold which had been lent him at usurious rates of interest, he was forced by the European powers to accept British and French financial "advisors" in his government. The British soon succeeded in gaining political and military control of the country as well.

The 20th Century
During the First World War, Egypt's strategic position was crucial to the British, and Cairo was the staging-point for the Allied offensive which wrested Palestine, Arabia and Syria from Ottoman control. Even before the Ottoman Empire fell, Egypt's British governors

had declared the puppet khedive's independence from his Turkish sovereign. Prince Fuad styled himself King of Egypt when he came to the throne in 1917, but real power was still in the hands of foreigners.

After the war, nationalist sentiments crystallized in the Wafd party, led by Saad Zaghloul Pasha. When free elections for a Chamber of Deputies were held in 1924, the anti-British Wafd won a large majority of seats. It continued to be the prime nationalist force for decades afterwards.

The Second World War brought renewed military importance to Egypt. In 1940 an Italian invasion force from Libya pushed deep into Egypt before being turned around by British Empire troops. In the following year General Rommel and an army of trained desert fighters recaptured the ground and rolled swiftly into Egypt. They were stopped at El Alamein, only 60 miles from Alexandria, in 1942. By the end of the year the tide of war had turned in favour of the Allies, and Egypt was again securely in British hands.

King Farouk had come to the Egyptian throne in 1936, a handsome and promising youth trained in a British officers' school. Despite his good intentions, Farouk soon succumbed to the oriental atmosphere of palace intrigue and luxurious living. Government suffered, and military defeat in Palestine (1948) was followed by diplomatic defeat when the king tried to claim full control over the Sudan and the Suez Canal. Unrest grew, until he was overthrown in 1952. A group of military officers led by General Mohammed Naguib took over. After a short time, Naguib was replaced by the real mastermind of the revolution, Colonel Gamal Abdel Nasser.

The country was declared a republic on 18th June, 1953, and Nasser remained in power for 17 years. Despite his authoritarian rule, it was during this period that Egypt regained a sense of national identity: under an Egyptian-run government the country rapidly emerged as a leader of the Third World nations and started to overhaul and modernize the economy. The symbol for this effort became the Aswan High Dam whose giant power stations generate huge quantities of electricity supplying all of the country's needs.

When President Sadat succeeded Nasser in 1970, his more moderate influence provided the counter-balance the country so desperately needed.

Immense power of the Nile churns out millions of kilowatts (Aswan).

Egypt's energy and resources had been continually under strain as a result of the recurrent wars with Israel. In 1948, 1956, 1967 and 1973 hostilities had broken out between the two countries. It was under Sadat that the historic peace treaty between Egypt and Israel was finally agreed upon in 1979. Whatever one's political views, his courage and integrity have been admired by men of reason everywhere.

From ancient pharaohs to modern statesmen, from kings and queens, generals and rulers of every description Egypt's destiny has been formed and handed down from generation to generation through the ages. Ultimately though, the country's future rests with those whose roots stretch far back through 5,000 years of history—the Egyptian people.

23

Where to Go

Cairo

Founded where the Nile valley widens into the flat, fertile delta, Cairo has been at the centre of Egyptian life for 1,000 years. It's the largest city in Africa (pop. 8,500,000), and one of the most densely populated places on earth. Here, by the side of the slow, silent-flowing Nile a bewildering multitude of people live together in an intense bustle of excitement and activity.

The heart of the modern metropolis lies on the east bank of the Nile and extends onto the two islands of Gezira and Roda. Large luxury hotels rise on the river's banks in this area, and Garden City's cooling greenery stretches along the waterfront. No less than four bridges span the waters between the towering landmark of the Television Building to the north and Roda Island in the south. One of the busiest of these is Tahrir Bridge, which crosses the main branch of the river from Gezira Island to enter the very heart of the city, Tahrir Square.

Microcosm of Cairo's daily life, **Tahrir Square** throbs and rumbles all day long and half the night as well. The tremen-dous traffic roundabout is topped by an elevated circle of pedestrian walkway which is thronged incessantly. Pedlars and vendors take up time-honoured battle-stations each morning, waiting for the day's army of potential customers to hurry by—perhaps a million of them. In open spaces here and there, long queues of Cairenes with endless patience wait phlegmatically for overstuffed buses—in which there's often no room for them—to arrive and depart.

Tahrir Square is surrounded by several of Cairo's prestigious institutions: the **Egyptian Museum** (see p. 38), the Ameri-can University, the Ministry of Foreign Affairs, and the Nile Hilton. Leaving the square, Talaat Harb street leads you to the beginning of Cairo's chic shopping and business street,

Mightiest of African rivers is the silent soul of modern Cairo.

Kasr El-Nil. Cinemas, cafés, restaurants and tea-shops abound in these thoroughfares, providing refuge from the bustle of daytime commerce. At night the main streets are brightly lit and thronged with strollers, window-shoppers, and young people on their way to the theatre or cinema. If the excitement becomes overpowering, escape to the Nile-side promenade of Cairo's Corniche, due west of any point in the city centre.

Islamic Cairo

Wherever you go in Cairo, above the jumble of rooftops rises the fantasy architecture of mosques, domes and minarets. The city preserves a rich tradition of Islamic artistry, and even the darkening caused by time cannot rob these imaginative structures of their charm. Go east from Tahrir Square passing by the large 19th-century Republic (Abdin) Palace to get to Ahmed Maher Square, and thence through a busy market area to the massive cylindrical bastions of **Bab Zuweila,** an imposing gate in Cairo's medieval city walls. Many a condemned criminal or opponent of the ruler was hanged from this gate in times past.

The two minarets on top of the gate actually belong to the adjoining **mosque,** finished in 1420 by the Mameluke Sultan El-Moayyad. This sultan's political enemies had him held prisoner in Bab Zuweila's infamous prison. While he was there he swore to build a mosque if he ever got free of them. When he did, he designed a particularly beautiful one which has outstanding stonework and a pretty garden in its courtyard. Have the caretaker show you the *mashna'a* (prison), and the stairway to the top of Bab Zuweila—there's a marvellous view.

From here walk north along the street named Muizz lidinillah and bear right to reach **El-Azhar Mosque and University,** Islam's most prestigious place of learning. Its Arabic name means "The Splendid", and there can be little doubt that its lofty gates and fairytale minarets capture the essence of Islamic architectural bravura. Begun in 970, the original Mosque of Fatima ez-Zahra was later expanded with libraries, hostels for pilgrims and students, gates and minarets. Pass through the sunny courtyard, lined with hostel rooms

Slender minaret thrusts heavenwards, marking a Cairo mosque. When visiting, remove your shoes.

(rwak) to the Great Chamber *(liwan)* for a look at the two prayer niches. El-Azhar is still a university as in medieval times, but today 20,000 students from all over the Islamic world come here to study medicine and law as well as theology.

Cross the tumultuous traffic in Gohar el-Qaid Street to reach Cairo's renowned handicrafts bazaar, **Khan el-Khalili.** A shopping trip to Khan el-Khalili is a must for any visitor to Egypt (see also page 84), and yet this is not a tourist market in a strict sense. The tiny shops, selling everything from priceless oriental jewellery to cheap gimcracks and household items are thronged with Cairenes as well as visitors: a gold bangle for a newborn baby girl, a silken caftan for a fiancée, or rare coins for investment are all eagerly sought out.

What would your friends say if you brought a hubble-bubble home?

Many of the shops are themselves works of art, boasting ornate doorways of carved wood and delicate traceries, floors covered in oriental carpets, and interiors perfumed with the scent of cedar, sandalwood or incense. Ask the shopkeeper for a tour of his workshops, and he will lead you on a labyrinthine chase to a crumbling room at rooftop level where men and boys are hard at work. Intricate inlay work, pounded copper, or jewelled arabesques in silver or gold are produced before your eyes. When you see what is involved in making one of these handicraft items, you'll realize that Khan el-Khalili prices are really quite moderate.

Return to Muizz lidini-llah to get to the imposing **Kalawun Mosque** complex, including a *maristan* (hospital), *madrassa* (theological seminary), the mausoleum of Sultan Kalawun, and the mosque itself. The complex was finished in 1293. Its façade is richly worked in the Islamic style, but somehow curiously reminiscent of Crusader architecture brought from France. Be sure to visit the **sultan's mausoleum.** At the end of a dingy passageway, a right turn reveals a magnificent towering portal leading to a great chamber of breathtaking beauty. The carved and gilded ceiling is par-

ticularly fine, an outstanding example of the Moslem craftsman's art.

In the adjoining building, rivalling Sultan Kalawun's pomp, is the **Madrassa of Sultan Berquq** dating from 1386. As you pass the finely worked bronze doors you'll find yourself gazing up at a canopy covered in gold arabesques on an azure background. Give the caretaker a small tip, and he'll open a door for you to see the nicely decorated tomb of Sultan Berquq's daughter.

Though it's only a short stroll from Berquq's Madrassa to your next stop, the Musafirkhana, a guide is essential to lead you through the maze of narrow streets. Ask any neighbourhood child, he'll be only too pleased to help. **Musafirkhana** (Turkish for "guest house") is a well-preserved mansion built in Mameluke style towards the end of the 18th century. The intricately carved ceiling in the main salon is strikingly attractive, and other graceful features such as the small private interior court recall a leisurely and refined way of life.

Find your way back to Muizz lidini-llah to see the tiny **El-Aqmar Mosque** (1125), ruined except for its unusual façade. A few steps north and to the right is **Bayt es-Suheimi**, home of a sheik who was rector of El-Azhar two centuries ago. His house was divided into the traditional sections of *salamlik*, where male guests were received, and *haremlik*, the private family quarters in which his wife and daughters lived. Off the main reception room is a chamber with huge chairs—symbols of the sheik's importance. Upstairs in the *haremlik*, stained glass, Turkish tiles, and the turned wooden screens *(mousharabiyeh)* change the women's "prison" into a palace.

Approaching the northern wall of medieval Cairo, the great **Mosque of El-Hakim** stands out on the right. The mosque was finished in 1013 by the infamous mad caliph, El-Hakim, and though age has brought down its roof and destroyed much decoration it is still vast and impressive.

Nearby, the gates of Bab Futuh and Bab en-Nasr were part of the **city walls** constructed at the end of the 11th century. These early walls have been much mended and rebuilt over the years, but principally by Napoleon's troops less than two centuries ago. The names which soldiers carved into the stones of the towers and bastions can still be read. A guide will appear from nowhere to sell you a ticket, lead you up to the top of the wall, and show you where the town's defenders performed the malodorous but devilishly effective task of pouring boiling oil down on the heads of attackers.

The Citadel

From the centre of Cairo, the approach to the Citadel is between two very noteworthy mosques. **Sultan Hassan Mosque** was a triumphal achievement for its royal builder, who finished it in 1362. The extreme height and austere grandeur of the main portal are matched inside by four cavernous *liwans* (covered prayer areas) inspired by the Persian-Turkish tradition. The **Tomb of Sultan Hassan,** behind the *mihrab* (prayer niche), has pretty stained glass windows, a band of inscription along its walls, and striking squinches supporting the dome. The tomb itself is of Egyptian alabaster.

Across the road, the **Rifai Mosque** was finished in 1912 and used as a final resting-place for scions of the house of Mohammed Ali. In fact, only Kings Fuad (1868–1936) and

Sultan Hassan Mosque: a fountain provides for ritual ablutions.

32

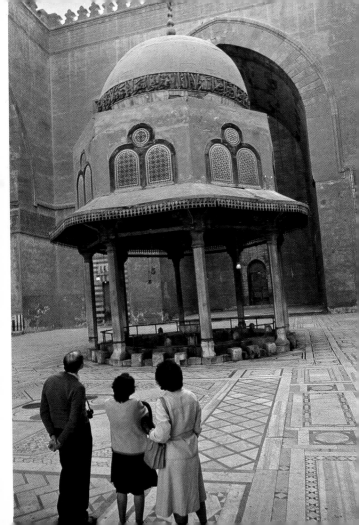

Farouk (1920–1965) are entombed here.

Take the road up to the **Citadel,** a Crusader-style fortress dating from the time of Saladin (1207). As you pass through the mammoth walls, think of what it must have been like for the Mameluke notables who came to "dine" at Mohammed Ali's invitation in 1811. That night the Pasha sat down to dinner alone knowing full well that all his rivals had been quietly and efficiently dispatched a few hours earlier (see p. 21).

The most eye-catching of the Citadel's buildings is the **Mosque of Mohammed Ali** ("Alabaster Mosque"). The style is Ottoman Baroque, with a few dashes of Louis Philippe. The mosque's plan is Turkish, with a large open forecourt surrounded by a colonnade. Even the pharaohs did not use alabaster as lavishly as Mohammed Ali did: the whole interior is covered in the creamy stone, though the Pasha had his own tomb (to the right as you enter) made from Carrara marble.

Go around behind the mosque when you leave it for a **panoramic view** of Cairo and the Nile. If it's not too hazy, you'll see the pyramids in the distance, poised at the edge of the desert. Before leaving this observation spot, search the jumble of city blocks for the large square court and ziggurat minaret of Ibn Tulun Mosque, a short distance west of the Citadel. It's your next stop.

Though a few Cairo mosques may be older, **Ahmed Ibn Tulun's** is the best-preserved of the city's very early (879) Islamic structures. Its court is the largest in Cairo, enclosed by a deep porch held up by five arcades. Next door to the mosque is one of Cairo's most fascinating museums, **Gayer-Anderson House,** a pair of traditional Arab houses joined together and filled with works of art both oriental and western. Major Gayer-Anderson, an English officer, bought these two houses (which date from 1540 and 1631), restored them, and lived here between the World Wars.

Jumble of modern buildings surround ancient Tulun Mosque.

Besides being splendid examples of traditional domestic architecture, the museums are a good place to see Persian, Turkish, Arabic, European, and even Chinese decorative arts. The Islamic Museum administers Gayer-Anderson House, which is open during normal museum hours (see p. 116).

(see p. 116)

Sand-colour by day, Cairo blazes in polychrome brilliance at night; Landmark tower is El-Borg, Gezira.

Old Cairo

Old Cairo is a few miles south of the modern city's centre, reachable by taxi or—if you don't mind a bit of crowding—by commuter train from Bab el-Luq Station near Falaki Square. Leave the train at the Mari Girgis stop.

Long before the founding of modern Cairo, it was here that the Romans had a fortress called Babylon. The entrance to the old city is between two bulky Roman towers. Once inside the walls, you are surrounded by Coptic churches and monasteries dating back to the time when Egypt was a Christian country. **El-Moallaqah,** "The Suspended Church", gets its unusual name from being built on top of two towers of a Roman city gate with its mid-part "suspended" between them. Its foundations date from the 7th century but evidence seems to suggest that there was a church even in the 4th century. It claims to be the oldest church in Egypt, but then so does **Abu Serga Church.** At this latter, according to legend, Mary, Joseph and the infant Jesus took shelter during their flight into Egypt. Abu Serga is deep in the back streets of Old Cairo which are lined with venerable doorways and paved with big stone blocks smoothed by centuries of wear. Glance upward as you walk along, and behind the *mousharabiyeh* screens on the windows you'll notice at least a dozen pairs of eyes watching your every movement with fascination and delight.

Just a few steps from Abu Serga is the **Church of Saint Barbara,** decorated in typical Coptic style. Next door to it on the right is the small **Synagogue Ben-Ezra.** The caretaker is proud of his little-known house of worship, and will show the congregation's very old holy books if you contribute to the upkeep of the synagogue.

Before leaving Old Cairo, pay a visit to the **Coptic Museum** (see page 40).

Two Islands

To escape from the exhausting frenzy of the city's busy streets, head for **Gezira** with its sporting clubs, parks and the **Cairo Tower** (El-Borg). A pretty tea-garden at the tower's base is just right for a rest and a refreshing cool drink. Afterwards, whisk to the top of the 600-foot tower for a marvellous view from the observation deck, and perhaps a dish of ice-cream at the snack bar on the floor below. Take your camera, and pick a clear day for your visit.

Roda Island, slightly smaller than Gezira, holds Mohammed Ali's **Manial Palace,** now a museum (see page 41), in its northern reaches. Also in the north is the Meridien hotel, while at the southern tip you'll be able to see Cairo's **Nilometre** (El-Miqyas), set up in the year 715 to give a clear indication of when the river would be at full flood. Now, due to the Aswan High Dam's careful control of the Nile's waters, the Nilometre has become obsolete.

the centre of Cairo, Tahrir Square, the **iseum** is one of the st important in the country. Constructed in the middle of the 19th century by the khedive Abbas Hilmi, its purpose was to house the wealth of artefacts discovered as a result of the wave of enthusiasm for Egyptology, started off by the French military and cultural invasion. Today, the museum preserves a scholarly character and Egyptologists love it: every single piece is on display and bears a catalogue number. The vastness of the collection is such that, if time is short, it's advisable to concentrate on the best items rather than trying to see everything fleetingly.

Turn left after handing in your ticket and walk between pairs of colossal statues to the Old Kingdom room harbouring the most ancient statues and sarcophagi. A small funerary chamber from Dahshur (Desheri, 6th Dynasty) has colourful engraved walls on which are noted the supplies provided the dead man for his celestial voyage, including a few jugs of beer to quench a powerful Egyptian thirst.

Farther along, you'll be struck by the stylized but still intensely life-like statue (No. 141)

of a scribe from Saqqara (5th Dynasty), its glass eyes catching glints of light with startling reality. In Room 32, the realistic statues of High Priest Ra-Hotep and his wife Nofret (No. 223) are plain evidence that the ancient Egyptians were very beautiful, and knew how to make the most of their gifts with cosmetics and clothing. The artists' magic was not reserved exclusively for humans as No. 446 (in Room 12) proves: the beautifully serene cow effigy is a symbol of the goddess Hathor. It was found "living" in the shed behind it, which comes complete with its own starry firmament. In Room 8, the gilded coffin lid set with carnelians and blue glass was made for Tutankhamon's brother. Room 3, devoted to the reign of Akhenaton, has two giant statues of the king in the exaggerated naturalistic style of the period, showing a distended belly and enormous effeminate thighs. They are very grotesque but impressive.

Upstairs above the Old Kingdom room are dozens of mummy cases exquisitely decorated both inside and out. Buy a ticket at the booth to pay your respects to their wizened occupants, who now repose in the Mummy Room. The mummies look a bit the worse for wear, but it is still astounding to see that even after some 3,500 years they are so well-preserved that one can imagine how they looked in life, even down to their carefully plaited hair.

For a look at the daily activities of ancient Egyptians, Rooms 22, 27, 32 and 37 are the ones to visit. The delightful little wooden figures which fill these rooms were made as "servants" for the dead, to provide for the honoured departed in the next life. Soldiers, boatmen with a funeral ship, craftsmen with toy tools, even ducks, fish, dogs and cattle—whole villages of wooden figures—were found all together. Daily life along the Nile in pharaonic times was obviously busy and varied, whether in this life or the next.

Prepare yourself for a thrill when you enter the section specially reserved for the display of **King Tutankhamon's treasures.** The king died mysteriously at the tender age of 19 years. His half-finished tomb in the Valley of the Kings at Thebes (Luxor) was filled with an array of treasure unparalleled in its variety, exquisite beauty, and sheer weight of gold. Seeing this treasure of

King Tut's funeral mask: a flawless treasure for a minor king.

1,700 items buried with an unimportant king, who can even imagine what the tombs of great and long-lived pharaohs such as Ramesis II must have contained? But only Tutankhamon's escaped the ravages brought by centuries of grave-robbing, to be found intact in 1922 by an English archaeologist named Howard Carter.

In Room 4 are the best of the "smaller" pieces, including a solid gold coffin, much jewellery, and Tutankhamon's famous mask, considered by many to be one of the most beautiful objects in the world. The treasure fills the corridors and galleries near Room 4 as well: gold-plated cases, one of them large enough to garage a small car; the king's exquisite bejewelled golden throne, bearing the sun-symbol of Aton (whom the king later forsook, turning back to worship of Amon); and a large golden box surmounted by rows of sacred cobras *(uraeus)* and guarded by four comely gilded maidens. When you visit Tutankhamon's tomb in the Valley of the Kings (see p. 72), you will marvel that all this treasure could have been fitted into such a small underground room.

Just off Place Ahmed Maher, next to the Egyptian Library, is the **Museum of Islamic Art.** You'll be surprised at the variety of things made by Moslem craftsmen, including fine prayer mats, stained glass, inlaid stone work, mosque lamps, faience and illuminated manuscripts. The arms collection alone is worth visiting to see rifles and siege guns worked in silver, daggers and swords set with precious stones, and deadly-looking poignards, scimitars and yataghans. Remember as you tour the collections that Moslem artists were forbidden by the Koran to portray any being with a soul. Obviously, there were lapses in the strict observance of this rule.

Centrepiece of Old Cairo is the **Coptic Museum.** Fine examples of Coptic craftsmanship found in old churches and houses have been assembled here, especially carved wood, stained glass, *mousharabiyeh* screens and sculpted works. At first it looks very similar to Islamic work: the same delicate tracery used to illuminate Moslem holy books is found in Coptic Bibles as well. But the difference is soon apparent. Christian craftsmen were allowed by their religion to portray men and beasts. Coptic art is Egyptian Islamic art with the prohibitions removed and the artist unfettered.

Cairo's Museum of Islamic Art: a permanent collection open to all.

Mohammed Ali's palace on Roda Island became a museum shortly after the fall of the monarchy. In the **Manial Palace Museum,** you'll find pavilions and salons filled with the luxuries and curiosities of royal daily life, from lustrous Turkish tiles and carpets to sparkling jewels and chandeliers. Though the contents are worth a king's ransom, dust disguises much of their charm. If the palace becomes dreary, you have only to walk outdoors into the gardens to regain a sense of liveliness. The banyan trees, by the way, are over a century old.

At Professor Hassan Ragab's **Papyrus Institute,** in a houseboat on the Nile near the Sheraton Hotel, you can see papyrus being made and buy the finished product bearing a painting or drawing. Professor Ragab spent many years of research to discover exactly how the ancient Egyptians made papyrus. Much cheaper than animal-skin parchment and less cumbersome than clay tablets, the invention of papyrus was a major advance for civilized record-keeping.

For museum opening hours see page 116.

For museum opening hours see page 116.

41

Excursions from Cairo

Pyramids of Giza

Free of Cairo's intense traffic, cars to Giza rocket along the Avenue of the Pyramids. It's impossible to lose your way, for the road is dead straight and the centre divider is planted with ornamental bushes trimmed in the shape of pyramids. After only a few minutes' driving, Giza's wonders of the world loom before you. The Empress Eugenie of France was the first to have admired this view of the pyramids when she inaugurated the Avenue in 1869. She had come to Egypt for the opening of the Suez Canal.

The pyramids are right at the edge of the modern city, and also right on the verge of the desert. The geometrical shapes, so perfect from a distance, yield their secrets of construction as you approach them. Each is made from millions of massive stone blocks, and their faces are in fact like giant staircases, not smooth as they first appear to be. With no doors or windows to give them scale, the monolithic forms seem deceptively small until you arrive at their bases. Then, these man-made mountains overpower you with their ponderous, precise majesty.

The **Great Pyramid of Cheops,** largest of the three, is 450 feet (137 metres) high and is made of nearly 2½ million gigantic stone blocks. Many visitors clamber to the top for a look at the city and the Nile, though this is supposedly forbidden. (Climbing the pyramids can be hazardous as a number of deaths in recent years have demonstrated.) As for a visit to the interior of the Great Pyramid, only the fairly athletic and non-claustrophobic should follow the guide into the spooky depths for a look at Cheops' funerary chamber, complete with sarcophagus and ventilation shafts.

Camel-drivers in the area are ever-ready to hoist you onto their ungainly beasts—who kneel co-operatively—for the short ride between pyramids. For those who prefer comfort to adventure, several horsecarts are also available for hire.

The **Pyramid of Chephren** is actually only a foot or two lower than the Great Pyramid, but as it's built on higher ground it looks taller from a distance. The covering of smooth-finished stones, once a feature of almost all the pyramids, can still be seen near Chephren's top. You can penetrate into the heart of this man-made mountain too, but do so only with a guide.

Pyramids

The ideas that first prompted the ancient Egyptians to start burying their dead under mounds are shrouded in the mystery of time. But whatever the original motives, from these first early piles of earth covered in bricks, came to be developed some of the most astounding structures ever constructed by man. (It is said that 100,000 men laboured for 20 years to build the Great pyramid of Cheops).

The earliest pyramids, called *mastabas*, were basically rectangular. When Imhotep put several *mastabas* one on top of the other for King Zoser's tomb the idea caught on and the era of pyramid construction began. Many of the mammoth monuments seem uncomplicated in their basic architecture (see below). In fact, the simplicity conceals a whole world of intricate design intimately related to the religious beliefs of the early Egyptians.

Cheops' Pyramid

1. Shafts
2. Gallery
3. Entrance
4. King's chamber
5. Queen's chamber
6. Underground chamber

The third and smallest **Pyramid of Menkure** (Mykerinos) is 204 feet (66 metres) high and was the last of the three Giza pyramids to be built. Notice the temples and tombs called *mastabas,* built all around the three great pyramids. They were put here so family, friends and noble servants of the pharaohs could be near their sovereign. All this impressive building was done in the times of the Old Kingdom's 4th Dynasty, about 2600 B.C. Scores of pyramids, earlier and later, line the Nile

Stele tells of early repairs to world's most enigmatic monument.

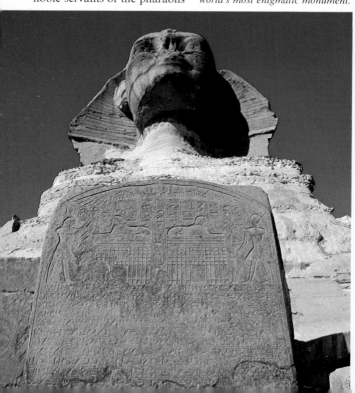

but those of Cheops, Chephren and Menkure are the finest of all.

The **Sphinx**—Abu el-Houl, or "Father of Fear" in Arabic—was sculpted in the image of Pharaoh Chephren as a guard for his pyramidal tomb. Some 1,000 years after the Sphinx was made, the ever-shifting desert sands had covered it completely. Thutmose IV (1425-08 B.C.) cleared the sand away and restored the great beast, according to an inscription on a stele which stands between its paws. After another 3,000 years the Mamelukes used the monument as a target for gunnery practice, thereby carrying out the Islamic prohibition against graven images while simultaneously improving the skills of their cannoneers. Recently, times have turned in the Sphinx's favour, and it is very well looked after by the Department of Antiquities.

Near the Sphinx, the funerary **temple of Chephren** is remarkable for the size and smoothness of its granite blocks and for its floor, made of alabaster. Another curiosity in the pyramids' complex is the **solar barque,** one of several long boats made of Lebanese cedar which were buried in deep pits next to the Great Pyramid. The boat, meant for use by Cheops on his celestial journey to the Other World, is kept in a small museum on the southern side of the Great Pyramid.

Saqqara and Memphis

Skirting fields watered by canals from the Nile, the road south from Giza leads to **Saqqara,** the largest necropolis in Egypt, with hundreds of tombs and monuments erected throughout the length of ancient Egyptian history. Activity here was especially intense during the Old Kingdom, when pharaohs had their capital at Memphis, close by.

Look first at the **Step Pyramid of Zoser** (or Jeser, 3rd Dynasty) the very earliest of the great pyramids built perhaps a century before those at Giza. King Zoser's architect, a nobleman named Imhotep, put all his ingenuity to work when designing this memorable tomb for his royal patron. Originally called *mastabas,* Egyptian tombs were rectangles more or less modified to suit the tastes and budget of the builder and future occupant. But Imhotep stacked six large *mastabas* of diminishing size on top of one another to create the Step Pyramid. The idea was a great success and a later king, Seneferou (4th Dynasty), also had a pyramid constructed at Dahshur, visible from Saqqara to the south. Seneferou's pyramid abandoned steps in favour of a standard base capped with a small, roof-like pyramidal top. This combination produces a bottom-heavy visual effect making the pyramids sides look "bent" when viewed from below. It was Seneferou's son Cheops who perfected the design and constructed the most impressive pyramid of all at Giza.

Near Giza pyramids, a son follows in his father's footsteps. (Right: Kagemni Tomb, Saqqara).

Of the tombs surrounding the Step Pyramid, several are graced with murals of exceptional beauty. The **mastaba of Princess Idut** (6th Dynasty) is at the end of the colonnade which you approach just after buying your entry ticket. It is particularly rich in nautical scenes. Next to it is the small **Pyramid of Unas** (5th Dynasty), and visible in the distance from this point are the Dahshur pyramids, including Seneferou's "bent" one.

North-east of the Step Pyramid, the **Tomb of Mereruka** (6th Dynasty) has 30 rooms decorated with scenes of hunting and fishing so exact in their detail that zoologists could use them to study the wildlife of ancient Egypt. The **Tomb of Kagemni** (6th Dynasty), next to that of Mereruka, has a number of equally fine murals, but with more of the colour preserved.

A short drive or walk to the north-west of the Step Pyramid brings you to the Rest-House named after Auguste Mariette, the French Egyptologist who discovered many of the monuments in this area. Camel-drovers will trot you from the Rest-House across the sands on their beasts (or you can walk the short distance) to the **Tomb of Ti** (5th Dynasty). This most

breathtakingly beautiful of Old Kingdom tombs was buried by desert sands for 4,500 years until uncovered by the ever-curious Mariette. Lord Ti was a high court official under several pharaohs, a powerful man who chose the finest craftsmen and artists to embellish his elaborate tomb.

Just north of Ti's tomb, you can see the **Serapeium** also discovered by Mariette in 1850–51. Sacred bulls were buried here from the earliest period of Egyptian civilization right up to the time of Christianity.

On the way back to Cairo, you can detour to the ruins of **Memphis** on the Nile, though there is little left of the great metropolis which remained the first city of Egypt until the end of the 6th Dynasty (about 2200 B.C.). A colossal, recumbent limestone statue of Ramesis II and an alabaster sphinx—which actually date from New Kingdom times—are all that recall ancient Memphis. The gigantic red granite statue of Ramesis II which once stood here is now next to the railway station in Cairo's Ramesis Square.

Alexandria
(Pop. 2,259,000)

About 220 kilometres by motorway (expressway) or train from Cairo is Alexandria. Founded by Alexander the Great in 332 B.C., this city has lived through fabulous times, though today little is left of its greatness except memories. Modern buildings crowd and cover antique ruins, and the polyglot internationalism of the 19th-century Levantine port has all but faded away. Many Cairenes spend part of their summer holidays in this Mediterranean resort although there are also a large number who are content to stay in Cairo and flip the switch on an air-conditioner.

You can easily visit Alexandria's sights in a day, and still have time for a swim. Start at the western end of the sweeping

Corniche named 26 July Street. It's the main waterfront thoroughfare and surrounds the eastern harbour. The coast road continues from the centre of town along the beach all the way to Montazah Palace 8 kilometres to the east. The peninsula at the Corniche's western end holds the former royal palace of Ras El-Tin.

Just east of the palace, part of the 15th-century Fort of Qait Bey now serves as a Naval Museum. It stands on the site of Alexandria's ancient Pharos, the elaborate lighthouse which was one of the wonders of the ancient world. Today, there's not much left of the lighthouse which flashed its warning in the age of the Ptolemies.

South of the Qait Bey Fort just a block from the Corniche stands the **Mosque of Abul Ab-** bas (1767), Alexandria's most impressive. Continue to the centre of town to find **Tahrir Square.** Though this is the city's largest public square, it's less important to tramway-riders, bus passengers and café-sitters than **Saad Zaghloul Square** a few blocks farther east. Zaghloul Square is the place for all these activities, as well as being the bus terminus.

Turn inland for a visit to the **Greco-Roman Museum.** Despite its name, it holds a good number of pharaonic relics as well. Other fascinating reminders of the city's Greek and Roman past are the Roman amphitheatre at Kom ed-Dik, unearthed in 1963, and the nearby catacombs of Kom esh-Shugafa. The catacombs date from the early years of the Christian era, and preserve an unusual mixture of pharaonic and Roman decorative styles. **Pompey's Pillar,** in a little park not far from the catacombs, actually has nothing whatsoever to do with the redoubtable General Pompey. The 98-foot-high monument of rosy Aswan granite was erected for Emperor Diocletian in the 3rd century A.D., considerably after Pompey's time.

Alexandria's beaches start right in the centre of town, but the best are those to the east at **Maamoura, Montazah** and **Abukir.** The last of these, at the site of Nelson's victory over Napoleon's fleet in 1798, is now famous for its seafood restaurants.

West of Alexandria, the Mediterranean coast stretches some 500 kilometres to the Libyan frontier. There are several resorts along the way, all accessible by train, bus or inter-city "serveece" taxis. A particularly pleasant spot 25 kilometres from Alexandria is AL AGAMI. Beyond is EL-ALAMEIN, the dusty dirty hamlet which took on immense importance during the savage battles of 1942. Here you'll find vast cemeteries full of casualties from both the armies involved in the fighting. SIDI ABDEL RAHMAN, 20 kilometres beyond the town has a beautiful beach

and an excellent hotel. Even further west, 185 kilometres from El-Alamein, is MERSA MATRUH, Egypt's well-kept secret of a beach resort. This town busies itself with provincial government matters, desert commerce and Mediterranean fishing, but you can devote yourself to sun and surf on sparsely populated beaches.

The desert road between Alexandria and Cairo has little traffic and offers the opportunity of visiting the **Coptic**

monasteries in Wadi Natrun. After following the road 120 kilometres from Alexandria, turn right at the Rest-House to reach the monasteries, 10 kilometres from the main road.

High walls, great piety, and a simple, ascetic life are the things valued by the monks at the four monasteries of Deir Amba Bishoi, Deir es-Suryani, Deir Amba Baramos, and Deir Abu Makar. This latter was the most important of the ancient monasteries, giving the Coptic

Flags, fiacres and multilingual signs: nostalgic reminders of Alexandria's polyglot history.

church most of its early fathers. Monks have lived in seclusion here since the 4th century. Visitors are welcome to tour certain parts of the monasteries and to visit their churches. One leaves with a profound impression of the pious and austere life— one which is not without its beauties.

51

Fayyoum

Fayyoum is an immense oasis surrounded by the Western Desert. It's accessible from Cairo by train, car or bus in an hour's drive on a good, fast road.

The land in the Fayyoum area is flat, with lush fields tilled by bullock-drawn plough or men wielding primitive mattocks. Horsecarts piled high with cane, grass mats, fodder or passengers rumble over the roads, passing women swathed in flowing black robes with heavily laden baskets balanced expertly on their heads. Here and there a palm grove provides welcome shade, or a picturesque waterwheel of darkened wood creaks slowly around, lifting the life-giving water from a canal to irrigation troughs in the fields.

Medinet El-Fayyoum, capital city of the province, is a considerable town of some 200,000 people. Crocodilopolis was its name in former times as it was sacred to the crocodile-god

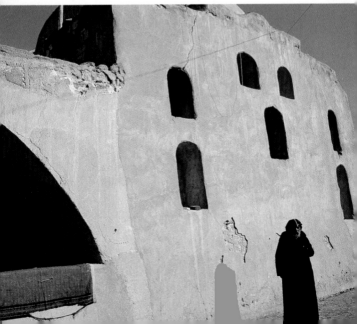

Sobek. Stop by Ain es-Syliin, a green park of mineral springs popular with day-trippers from Cairo who come to enjoy the pure air and greenery. Everybody takes bottles to fill with health-giving spring water for sipping back in the city.

Lake Qaroun, which occupies a large part of Fayyoum, used to fill it all. As it receded it left behind ric... which explains ... the region. The ... today is full of t... berge du Lac (n... mer) offers a pla... stay the night.

Of the pharaonic ruins in Fayyoum, those at **Medinet Madi** are the best-preserved and most extensive.

Venerable monks at Wadi Natrun (see previous page) have lived in pious austerity since Christianity began. Below: Fayyoum, a vast desert garden.

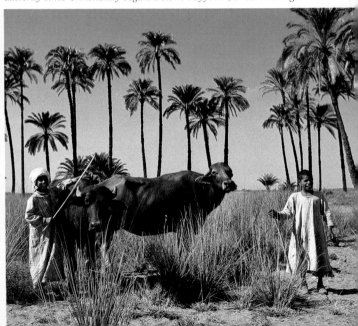

Egypt

As the slender green valley of the Nile meanders ever southwards, the Egypt of the Arabs is left behind giving way to the Egypt of the Africans. Lower Egypt's delta is vast and rich, but in Upper Egypt the fertile soil brought (until the building of the Aswan High Dam) by the mighty river, lines only a few hundred yards along either bank. The *fellahin* (peasant farmers) make up for the lack of land by intensive cultivation of the little they have. A journey south along the Nile here reveals green fields of sugarcane and cotton, with camels pulling primitive ploughs, turning waterwheels, or towing carts. Every sort of pumping system ever devised by man, simple or ingenious, is pressed into service to irrigate the fields.

Dotted along the Nile's banks are traces of pharaonic Egypt, from dusty heaps of broken pottery to magnificent temples. At Abydos, the votive **temple** to Osiris built by Seti I (19th Dynasty) has fine mural paintings, though you must step carefully in the shadowy rooms with their broken floors. (Bring a powerful light if you have one.) Abydos was a place especially sacred to the memory of Osiris, the well-loved earthly god who was murdered and cut into pieces by his brother. Unable to rule on earth, Osiris became king of the nether world. The sacred city built here in his honour disappeared long ago, but the great Seti temple, recently restored, remains an imposing monument.

The **Oseirion,** behind the temple, was a cenotaph for Seti I, who wanted to show his love of Osiris by having a tomb here, though he arranged for his true burial to be in the Valley of the Kings at Thebes.

Farther on, a five-minute walk across the sand brings you to the ruined **Temple of Ramesis II,** which still shows some traces of the bright colours which once blazed from its walls.

Continuing south on the river you come to the temple complex at **Denderah** (Tentyris). Many styles and periods of Egyptian art are brought together here, making Denderah a virtual museum of architecture. The **Mammisi* of Augustus** to the right after passing through the great gate was built in Roman times. The artistry of the reliefs is poor compared to the excellence of Middle and New Kingdom art. The fascinating scenes on the south

54

---

* birth-temple

wall and throughout the temple show the birth and nourishment of an infant god, meant to symbolize the Egyptian monarch. Another birth-temple, the Mammisi of Nectanebo (30th Dynasty) was built late in pharaonic times. Between the two Mammisi are the ruins of a Coptic church.

A pharaoh's life was filled with dazzling ceremony. Here he greets Hathor and Ra (Denderah).

Denderah's **main temple** is dedicated to Hathor, mother of the gods, wife of Horus. She is often portrayed as a beautiful woman whose head is topped by a pair of graceful horns bordering a solar disc. Sometimes she takes the shape of a fertile, genial cow, and sometimes she combines attributes of both woman and cow. The columns in the hypostyle hall are topped by capitals bearing the face of Hathor. The offertory hall has similar columns and in the murals Hathor is shown going about her benevolent business. Farther into the temple, the dingy and mysterious holy of holies is sombre and vaguely disquieting as you stand surrounded by mystical bas-reliefs and the dust of ages. The caretaker will take you down into the crypts for a look at several fine murals, but don't go if you're averse to stooping and scrambling, or to sharing the claustrophobic underground tunnels with bats.

Above the holy of holies are rooms with murals showing the Egyptian process of embalming, and ceilings framed by the sinuous body of the celestial goddess Nut, who symbolized the sky to ancient Egyptians. Up on the temple roof, the bright sunlight dispels the gloom of the holy of holies at once. Look for the Sacred Lake on the temple's western side. Behind the temple is the smaller Temple of Isis, sister and wife of Osiris, mother of Horus.

Divine Coexistence

Ancient Egypt's religion was a matter of divine profusion and confusion. Scores of local gods merged attributes with one another and with gods from other areas, and no one was ever quite sure which was which. All appear to have been happy and benevolent, and early Egyptians seem to have felt no pressing need to tidy up the pantheon. The simplified chart below may help you identify some of the most popular gods.

Deity	Forms	Function
Amon-Ra	Sun, ram, hawk	Chief god, patron of Thebes
Osiris	Pharaoh	Underworld god
Isis	Beautiful woman	Sister-wife of Osiris; Horus' mother
Hathor	Cow, goddess with horns	Fertility, love, joy
Horus	Falcon, winged solar disc, infant	Sun god, protector of the king; many other functions of deity
Anubis	Jackal	Funeral ceremonies god
Thoth	Ibis	Wisdom and learning
Ptah	Man	Creator, teacher of skills and crafts
Maat	Ostrich plume	Justice

Luxor

(Pop. 30,000)

From 2100 to 750 B.C. (the 10th to 25th Dynasties) the centre of Egyptian power and glory was focused in the temples of Luxor and Karnak in the city of Thebes. It was here that the New Kingdom (1570–1100 B.C.) saw its finest hour. While the city of the dead lay on the western bank of the Nile, the city of the living thrived between the two great temples.

But the fourteen centuries of Theban grandeur were brought abruptly to an end by the Assyrian invasion of Egypt in the 7th century B.C. and Thebes soon became only a crumbling but magnificent attraction for visiting Greeks and, later, Romans.

Then, renewed interest in the city saw Egyptologists sweeping away the dust of centuries from Theban temples and seeking

No adventure leaves lifetime memories like a cruise on the Nile.

the hidden entrances to pharaonic tombs. The mid-19th century opening of the Suez Canal increased European interest in Egypt, and visitors discovered the area's perfect and healthful winter climate. Tourists have been enjoying Luxor's temperatures, temples and tombs ever since.

The town's long riverside **Corniche** is bordered by trees and outdoor cafés, with Nile cruise boat docks dotted along the bank. Graceful feluccas tie up next to the tourist boats, hoping to take passengers for a water-borne view of the town, or to ferry them to the Valley of the Kings on the Nile's opposite shore. The great pillars of Luxor Temple, illuminated at night, dominate the eastern bank, and strollers staying on the boats or in the renowned Winter Palace Hotel never tire of passing this ancient monument. A week seems like a very short time to spend in this supremely pleasant place—half a week is barely enough to see the essential sights.

The most convenient spot to begin your sightseeing is at Luxor's **Great Temple.** This impressive building served as the setting for only one solemn pageant celebrated at the beginning of each new year, that of the chief god Amon. Amenophis III (18th Dynasty) and Ramesis II (19th Dynasty) contributed most to the construction of the temple during the period 1400–1250 B.C. When you visit it, let your imagination conjure up the ceremonies of Amon's procession, with the god symbolized in various forms, Amon-Ra, the Sun God, or as Amon-Min, the lascivious and outrageously demonstrative deity whose unmistakable phallic image appears in the temple's murals in several places.

In front of the great pylon, you'll see only one of the two finely wrought obelisks, which Mohammed Ali presented to France in 1831. The other was taken to Paris and now stands in the Place de la Concorde. Inside the great pylon up to the left, the little Mosque of Abu'l Haggag is perched on pillars in the court of Ramesis II. Several churches once shared the temple grounds as well. Past this court, a great colonnaded way, simple but enormous, leads to the older, inner court of Amenophis III.

At first it's difficult to imagine that the Luxor Temple was a "minor" one, but the short ride to the awe-inspiring temple in Karnak will bring you face-to-face with pharaonic Egypt's grandest monument of all. The **59**

Great Temple of Amon is actually the largest of a vast complex of temples, sacred lakes, chapels and sphinx-lined triumphal ways which filled nearly two miles along the Nile, from Karnak to the Luxor Temple. A century of archaeological work has uncovered and reconstructed a great deal, but there was so much built during the 1400 years of Theban greatness that the work may never be finished.

The Great Temple was built, modified and expanded according to pharaohs' whims over a period of 2,000 years from the Middle Kingdom to Roman times. The first part you see was the last part built: the towering and massive **first pylon,** largest in the world, was to have been the Ptolemies' contribution to the temple, but they never finished it. Its broad expanse was never carved to record the great moments of the Ptolemy dynasty. Behind the tremendous bulk of the 40-foot thick pylon is the largest **court** of any Egyptian temple, an open space of about 8,000 square yards. The Temple of Seti II (19th Dynasty) is the little shrine on the left as you enter. The one farther along on the right is the work of Ramesis III (20th Dynasty). The sacred barque, symbolizing the sun's journey through the celestial "sea" was mounted in a place of honour on the structure in the court's centre.

The second pylon, guarded by two colossal statues of Ramesis II, hides the most stupendous room in the ancient world: the **great hypostyle hall,** overpowering with its 134 gigantic columns, those along the central aisle being even taller than the rest. A surprising amount of the original paint and decoration is visible high up on the columns. Stand here a moment. It takes a period of time for the full effect of this huge room to sink in.

The third pylon, directly behind the great hypostyle hall, dates from the reign of Amenophis III (18th Dynasty, about 1400 B.C.). The narrow court between the third and fourth pylons held four fine granite obelisks, of which only one

In a corner of Karnak Temple, sphinx-like rams bask in the sun. **61**

remains, but an even bigger obelisk (one of a pair) erected past the fourth pylon by Queen Hatsheput is even better. The fourth and fifth pylons, erected by Thutmose I (18th Dynasty, about 1525 B.C.) are among the oldest parts of the temple.

Past the sixth pylon is the granite sanctuary which housed the sacred barques, and behind this is the very oldest section of the great temple, part of a modest shrine erected in Middle Kingdom times.

The ruined temple area is so vast, with piles of stones fallen here and there and hidden by high grass, that most of the structures which used to surround the temple are difficult to identify without an elaborate archaeological plan. But there is no missing the **Sacred Lake** just

---

Egyptian Temples

Though each great temple is slightly different, all have a similar masterplan. A mammoth gateway, or pylon, came first, and behind it was an open courtyard. A second pylon and a second courtyard followed. Next came a room called a "hypostyle", filled with columns to support a roof. Another such room might follow, sometimes called the hall of offerings. Finally, the inner sanctum, or "holy of holies", was where the god "lived" and where priests performed arcane ceremonies and sacred rites. A typical temple plan might look like this.

1. First pylon
2. Second pylon
3. Hypostyle hall
4. Hall of offerings
5. Holy of holies

south of the Great Temple of Amon. Part of the ceremonial at Amon's temple required setting the sacred barques afloat on the lake to symbolize the daily celestial journey of Amon-Ra, the Sun. Behind the lake to the east are seats for the evening sound and light show. At the northern corner of the Sacred Lake a man at a small and very un-pharaonic stand sells refreshing drinks, providing an excuse for a rest-stop.

In the late afternoon, Luxor's fine little **museum** north of the Etap Hotel opens its doors, and no visitor to Luxor should miss spending a pleasant half-an-hour in its air-conditioned rooms. Unlike the jumbled Egyptian Museum in Cairo, the Luxor Museum is small and the collection well selected and artfully displayed. The striding basalt statue of Thutmose III (No. 2) is particularly fine, and the striking, unusual sandstone bust of Amenophis IV (Akhenaton, No. 53) gives some appreciation of this exceptional pharaoh's strong character.

The best time for a stroll in the modern town of Luxor is at dusk when the market streets are still filled with life but not overcrowded. Most of the day's business has been done, and shopkeepers sit contentedly at their doors watching the passing parade. At sunset, it's pleasant to sit at a Nile-side café. One, with an upper-level terrace, between Luxor Temple and the New Winter Palace Hotel, has a fine view of the river and the temple.

Theban Necropolis

The Valley of the Kings shelters the fabulous tombs of many great Theban pharaohs, including the relatively modest one belonging to Tutankhamon. But the valley is only a small part of a vast "city of the dead" which extends over large tracts on the far (western) side of the Nile from Luxor. Including the tombs of countless nobles, court officers and royal family members, the number of burial-places is in the hundreds. A dozen temples, large and small, are scattered throughout the necropolis. An attempt to appreciate all this magnificence in a single day could well end in bewilderment and exhaustion, so it's a good idea to plan at least two days to tour the major sights of Thebes' City of the Dead.

Motorized ferry-boats ply the Nile between the Winter Palace dock, the Savoy Hotel dock, and the western bank. The boats are most active around 8 or 9 o'clock in the morning, and again at 4 o'clock in the afternoon, the hour when the tombs close for the day. The booth at the west bank dock is the place to buy your tickets to one or more of the temples and tombs. Don't set off to the tombs without them. Next to the booth, plenty of taxis, donkeys and bicycles are always available for hire.

From the dock, a road heads inland through lush irrigated farmland. About a mile and a half along, towards the ragged mountains, a pair of mammoth seated figures rise from the midst of a farmer's field: these are the celebrated **Colossi of Memnon.** The temple which must have enclosed them was ruined long ago by earthquakes, but these two seated figures of Pharaoh Amenophis III remain, giving mute testimony to the greatness of their maker more than 3,000 years after his death. Unlike most monuments in this region, the Colossi sit on priceless agricultural land, though the edge of the desert is only a few hundred yards away.

West of the Colossi is a complex of temples called by its modern Arabic name, **Medinet Habu.** A rough and crumbling mud brick wall surrounds two temples which seem, as you enter, to present a never-ending file of pylons. The first temple was started in the time of Ameno-phis I (18th Dynasty). It's very revealing to compare this small, pretty temple with the much larger one behind it, which is the work of Ramesis III (20th Dynasty), who lived some 350 years after Amenophis. The Ramesis temple was put up all at one time rather than over the centuries, and though its size is impressive, it is less pleasing aesthetically. Look closely at the relief decoration: it's carved very deeply to make it more dramatic, but the depth makes it seem somewhat coarse as well. The temple's plan is the classic one, though it has three hypostyle halls, and also an unexpected delight: a stairway concealed in its second pylon allows you to trudge to the top for a view of Medinet Habu, the fertile countryside and the rugged hills.

From Medinet Habu, a road runs directly to the **Valley of the Queens.** Close to 80 tombs here sheltered the remains of queens and royal children, though few have survived the ravages of time in good condition. Two are well worth a visit. Number 55, that of Amon-her-Khopeshef (or Amon-chopeshfu, 20th Dynasty) preserves very fine paintings with astonishingly bright colours, especially the blues and yellows. Then, the Tomb of Queen Nefertari, No.

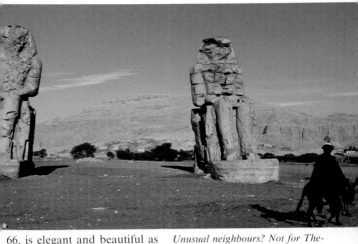

66, is elegant and beautiful as befitted the wife of Ramesis II. Carved from rock, it's scale rivals that of many kings' tombs.

Returning from the Valley of the Queens, take the first turning left to reach the necropolis of **Deir el Medineh.** Of the hundreds of tombs discovered within and around this modern-day village, No. 1 is of greatest interest. It belonged to Sennejem, a high official of the 19th Dynasty, and its paintings retain an amazing freshness of colour, looking as though they were completed yesterday. Be careful as you descend because the stairway is broken, and the rock-hewn entrance very small.

Unusual neighbours? Not for Theban farmers who see them every day.

Tomb No. 359, of Inherka (20th Dynasty) is very close to No. 1 and is filled with paintings of gorgeous sloe-eyed goddesses.

The kings of the 19th Dynasty were ambitious builders, and none more than Ramesis II (1298–1235 B.C.), whose awesome monuments are strewn throughout Egypt. His tomb in the Valley of the Kings is a little disappointing, but the funerary temple he built to his own memory at the edge of the cultivated land remains a stupendous architectural achieve-past four fine seated figures of the pharaoh in granite, to your left. Just after them is a great bulk of ruined stone which formed a colossus of truly incredible stature: this seated figure was 56 feet high and weighed over 2,200,000 pounds.

Behind the Ramesseum on the hillside is the necropolis called **Sheik Abd El-Gurnah,** after the present-day village there. All the tombs worthy of a visit are left from the 18th Dynasty, one of the old Egypt's most glorious periods. Be prepared for some delay. The tombs tend to be small but the crowds of visitors are just the opposite. Caretakers illuminate the tomb interiors by an ingenious juxtaposition of mirrors, reflecting a brilliant beam of sunlight into the darkness. But only a few people can be in one of the tombs at a time or the beam will be blocked.

The **Tomb of Nakht,** No. 52, is small but depicts all the Nile's abundance in its beautiful scenes of wine-making, fruit-gathering, and reaping. Nakht was an astronomer attached to the Temple of Amon. In the nearby **Tomb of Mena,** No. 69,

ment. Called the **Ramesseum,** it was a vast collection of palaces, temples and storerooms. Now, though much ruined, the scale of the temple and the score of huge statues in the image of Ramesis leave modern visitors with a vivid impression. The present entrance to the ruins takes you into the second court,

Sacred sunlight, put to work with a crude reflector, gives tantalizing glimpses of Theban gentility.

the colours are equally beautiful, though the mirror-light and the glass plates which protect the murals weaken their impact. The **Tomb of Sennefer**, No. 96, is a bit out of the way at the end of a longish stairway and through a small opening. The guide's lamp casts only a feeble light on the stylized grapevines and odd geometric shapes which decorate the tomb walls. During a moment of silence deep in the earth, Sennefer's tomb can inspire gloomy thoughts, even in the least superstitious of visitors.

The **Tomb of Rekhmere-Ra,** No. 100, is as magnificent as one might expect for an ex-mayor of Thebes. Murals show ambassadors from foreign countries bringing offerings of giraffes, leopards, baboons and monkeys, elephant tusks and produce. Other murals show vignettes of Theban daily life as men work in the fields or at their crafts, producing goods to be offered to the great Amon.

Ramose's tomb, No. 55, like Rekhmere-Ra's is also an imposing eternal resting-place. But his pharaoh, Amenophis IV (Akhenaton) carried out his religious revolution while work was in progress, and Ramose's tomb was abandoned unfinished when pharaoh and court moved down the Nile to Tell el-Amarna. The bas-reliefs in the tomb are exceptionally fine. Girls with delicate features and carefully plaited hair were carved with great care, and then abandoned unpainted. The effect is one of seemingly exquisite engravings rather than of bas-reliefs. A few figures are outlined in black—the first stage in the painting process—and these offer a contrasting beauty.

For yet another glimpse of Theban artistry, find the **Tomb of Mahu (Khaemhat),** No. 57. It is unusual in that it shelters several statues of its owner and of members of his family.

The artistic brilliance of the 18th Dynasty seen in these tombs stands out even more boldly in the temples of **Deir el-Bahari,** west of the main road. The story of Queen Hatshepsut, for whom one of the temples was originally meant, is a fascinating tale. If a pharaoh had no legitimate son to be his heir, he **68** often put forward one of his illegitimate sons and married him to one of his legitimate daughters, thereby strengthening the son's claim. This happened to Thutmose I, bastard son of Amenophis I. But Thutmose and his wife Ahmose had the same problem over again: no son. Thutmose II was therefore selected from among Thutmose I's numerous bastard sons, and was married to Hatshepsut, princess of the royal blood. As luck would have it, Thutmose II and Hatshepsut had only daughters, and the problem of a legitimate successor arose yet again. Thutmose II died in 1505 B.C., perhaps of chagrin over the plethora of princesses, and yet another illegitimate son became Thutmose III. But the new pharaoh was a mere boy, and so Queen Hatshepsut, his step-mother, acted as regent, consolidating all power in her own hands. She became used to wielding the royal crook and scourge, symbols of the pharaoh's authority, and even dressed and acted as though she were really the pharaoh even wearing the traditional stylized beard. Her rule as a man lasted 22 years before her death allowed Thutmose III to take his rightful place. Thutmose then had a brilliant reign lasting until 1450 B.C.

The **Temple of Hatshepsut** is

unique in all Egypt, being built as a series of terraces on a grand scale, with stark colonnades blending in with the grooved mountainside which rises behind the temple. Hathor is the honoured goddess here, and murals showing the sacred cow are everywhere. The rooms behind the colonnade on the second terrace hold well-preserved paintings. The ceiling in the Chapel of Hathor at the southwestern (left) end of the terrace is as starry and blue as any night-time Egyptian sky, and the yellow hues are bright as reflected sunlight.

On your way to the renowned Valley of the Kings, stop at **Gurnah** for a look at the funerary temple of Seti I (19th Dynasty), father of Ramesis II. Little is left of the temple's first two pylons and courts, but the hypostyle hall is filled with scenes showing Seti I and his ubiquitous son Ramesis II making offerings to Thebes' great god Amon.

Hieroglyphs

By the time Upper and lower Egypt were united in 3000 B.C., ancient Egyptians had an answer to their need for an alphabet: 24 simple-to-use pictorial letters. But temple priests and scribes soon turned this easy answer into a complex problem when they filled the hieroglyphic alphabet with some 700 signs and arcane symbols which only they could understand. The use of hieroglyphs died out at the end of the 4th century A.D., though the ancient Egyptian language continued to be spoken by Copts.

The art of reading hieroglyphic inscriptions remained a mystery for centuries until Napoleon's soldiers found the three-language Rosetta Stone in 1799. With the help of the Stone, Jean-François Champollion, a French scholar, cracked the hieroglyphic code and discovered that hieroglyphs can be written right-to-left, left-to-right, or up-and-down. You can easily tell which way, because the animals always stare toward the beginning of the sentence.

Kings and queens enclosed their names in "cartouches". Here are two famous royal monograms you may see in temples and tombs:

Cleopatra   Ptolemy

Valley of the Kings

The western bank of the Nile, closer to where the sun began its daily course through the nether world, was always the preferred place for tombs and pharaohs of the 18th, 19th and 20th Dynasties chose this forbidding rock valley for their eternal resting-place. Undisturbed by the annual rising of the Nile waters and hidden away in rock-hewn sepulchres with secret, sealed entrances, they were well fitted out for their underworld journey. Furnishings and costumes, mummified statues or carved figures to act as servants and concubines, as well as food and a variety of drinks were all carefully included in each tomb. The royal voyagers even had a detailed guidebook to the dangers of the celestial journey—a copy of the Book of the Dead was standard tomb equipment. At the end of the trip they would meet the divine Osiris who would enlist the aid of Anubis and Thoth, gods of funeral rights and of wisdom, in judging the new arrivals: a pharaoh's heart would be weighed in a balance against a

Rock-hewn tombs concealed many treasures. Right: King Tut lived—and died—amid golden splendour.

feather, and if it was not heavy with sin, the pharaoh would be admitted to a pleasant life in the land of Osiris. In the Kingdom of Egypt which he had just left, he would take on an aura of deity like a lesser Osiris, and his family and loyal subjects would worship him in his funerary temple.

A king began work on his elaborate tomb and funeral equipment as soon as he came to power. Despite this admirable lack of procrastination, many monarchs had the misfortune to die before all was ready. They were immediately sealed up in their imperfect tombs as all the country's best artisans and craftsmen marched off to begin work on the new king's tomb. Though tombs might be guarded for centuries, and the hidden entrances lost to living memory, the ingenuity of grave-robbers increased along with the richness of the spoils. In the thousands of years since the New Kingdom, thieves succeeded in finding and breaking into every tomb—except one.

As you walk up the crunching gravel path to the Rest-House, the **Tomb of Tutankhamon,** No. 62, will be right before you. Though the tomb is very modest—the king died unexpectedly and was buried in a hurry—it is the only pharaonic tomb ever discovered intact. The dazzling wealth of this single unimportant king makes it almost impossible to imagine the total extent of riches once secreted in this forbidding valley.

Sacred apes glower from the walls of Tutankhamon's small, simple tomb, and four shapely maidens are carved into his sarcophagus to protect him. The gilded mummy-case within the sarcophagus is now empty. The solid gold inner coffin holding the king's mortal remains has been moved to the Egyptian Museum in Cairo (see p. 40).

Perhaps the most splendid tomb in the Valley of the Kings is the **Tomb of Seti I,** No. 17, south of the Rest-House. The murals in the descending rooms and corridors are still of striking beauty and freshness though they're over 3,000 years old. The lowest room once held the king's massive alabaster sarcophagus: it is now in the Soane Museum in London. The semicylindrical vault over the sarcophagus-spot is painted as a blue sky with gods, goddesses and animals among the starry constellations. Seti's great tomb was unfinished when he died, as you can see from the wall paintings and excavation work in the lowest chambers.

Back down the path from Seti's tomb, keep to the left to reach the **Tomb of Ramesis III,** No. 11. A fine yellow-gold solar disc over the doorway leads to a corridor with many small side-chambers bearing interesting and unusual illustrations of daily crafts and labours. In one picture, two harpists sing the praises of Ramesis III before the gods, adding music to this frenzy of terrestrial and celestial activity.

The **Tomb of Horemheb,** No. 57, is only a few steps west of No. 11. The paintings here are particularly unusual, done on a dark background to achieve a heightened dramatic effect. In the last room, the artists had hardly even completed the preliminary sketches in red, when Horemheb was ready to start his trip to the land of Osiris.

Complicated rites and ceremonies awaited pharaoh in the Next World.

Follow the western (right-hand) path from Horemheb's tomb to get to No. 35, the **Tomb of Amenophis II,** which is at the end of it. The paintings in the tomb are plain and of subdued colour, but very finely done. The king's richly decorated sandstone sarcophagus is still in place.

You must do some climbing and scrambling to get to the **Tomb of Thutmose III,** No. 34. It is the farthest south from the Rest-House, along a narrow path and up a steel stairway, then down another stairway and through a tiny entrance. Its decoration is very plain, with colour used quite sparingly,

though the result is attractive.

Sixty-two royal tombs have been uncovered so far in the Valley of the Kings, but only a small number are worth a look. Repair and preservation work continues, and you should not be surprised if one or more tombs are closed temporarily when you visit.

After the hot and dusty tramp around the tombs, the cool, breezy terrace of the Rest-House beckons. Prices for coffee, tea or cold drinks are higher than need be, but after the thrill of exploring the valley's artistic riches, a few minutes' relaxation are essential to absorb the wealth of impressions.

Luxor to Aswan

On the way up-river, at **Esna,** 60 kilometres south of Luxor, you'll find the **temple** dedicated to Khnum, the god who created men and animals by moulding them from Nile clay. Centuries of daily life on this spot have raised the level of the ground so that the temple now lies well below street level. Villagers still tell the story of the archaeologists who discovered the capitals of ancient columns in the streets and how they suddenly realized that the capitals were still attached to their columns. Subsequent excavations revealed the hypostyle hall of a temple first built in the 18th

Living right next to things incredibly ancient never loses its thrill, as at Edfu Temple, above.

Dynasty, but completely reconstructed in the time of the Ptolemies and of the Romans, when Egyptian decorative art was in deep decline.

Farther along the river, midway between Luxor and Aswan, the large town of **Edfu** holds Egypt's best-preserved temple. Dedicated to Horus, the multiform god of the sun and planets, the hawk (symbol of the god) is prominent in its decoration. One reason the temple is so well preserved is that it was finished very late, only a few decades before Antony and Cleopatra held sway over Egypt. Take a horse-drawn carriage from the Nile's bank, and in five minutes it will bring you, bones still jangling, to the temple grounds.

The **Temple of Horus** has a huge pylon, almost as big as Karnak's. You can climb to its top by the stairway concealed inside. Thirty-eight columns surround the court, and a very fine granite statue of Horus stands guard over the entry to the first hypostyle hall. Every available surface is carved with hieroglyphs describing offerings to the god. In the very centre of the holy of holies is a great block of granite hollowed out as a sanctuary, with another block before it to bear the sacred barque. A modern copy of the barque itself is on view in the room directly behind the god's sanctuary. Other small chambers, lit only by tiny windows in the stone, preserve the sombre gloom. This is rarely seen in other temples which are often roofless, letting in the brilliant sunlight.

A modest restaurant near the entrance to the temple grounds provides refreshments and a cool place to sit. The parade of shoeshine boys, souvenir vendors and bright-eyed children passing by your table will provide more amusement than you'll ever need.

Continuing along the Nile, your first view of the temple at Kom Ombo will fill you with excitement. It stands right on the Nile's eastern bank, looking just like a Nile-side temple should look. Unique in all Egypt, **Kom Ombo Temple** is shared equally by two gods: Sobek, the crocodile god of Nile fertility, and Haroeris, the great winged solar disc. The first temple rose during the time of the 18th Dynasty, but virtually all you see was built much later under the Ptolemies in the three centuries before the birth of Christ.

Everything here is in pairs: double doorways lead into the great court and through the two hypostyle halls to a double sanctuary. To make the temple come alive, try to imagine the doorways fitted with their massive wooden doors, and the walls, columns and arches glowing with rich colours in the semi-darkness of the roofed interior.

To the right of the temple entrance is a small chapel dedicated to Hathor, now filled with

Breathtaking immensity of Kom Ombo: temple shared by two gods.

an unusual legacy: a stack of mummified crocodiles sacred to Sobek. North of the temple court a stone staircase descends in a spiral to the local Nilometre at the bottom of a circular well.

Sleepy Nubian town gets visitors. Rescued column hardly shows cuts.

Aswan

The sleepy town of Aswan awakened in the 1960s to a flood of foreign engineers who had come to plan construction of an immense dam across the Nile. The Aswan High Dam (Saad El-Ali) was built by teams of engineers from the Soviet Union who directed a crew of

35,000 Egyptians in the work. The electricity and flood control facilities that it provided brought profound changes to the economy and agriculture of the country. While not all of the results of its construction had been foreseen, as ecological experts are now beginning to fear, most agree that the be-nefits of the project outweigh the disadvantages. When the enormous dam was completed in 1972, the town changed character completely.

Once a smaller version of Luxor, a town of farmers, holiday-makers and archaeologists, Aswan became an industrial centre with factories for iron and steel, fertilizer chemicals, and sugar. Today, despite the changes all around it, the centre of town retains the same pleasant quality that once made it a favoured wintering spot for the late Aga Khan and other wealthy visitors. White-sailed feluccas, like great one-winged water birds, slip rapidly up and down the Nile, dodging among the islands. Horse carts stand at the entrances of hotels, waiting for tourists to climb in for a clip-clop ride among the eucalyptus, citrus and palm trees. The gold and grey of the desert hills is best at dawn, when the twitter of birds and braying of donkeys signal the beginning of yet another perfectly sunny day.

While you're here, go by taxi to the **High Dam** (about 10 kilometres from town). In the lotus-shaped monument to Soviet-Egyptian cooperation you can take a lift to the top for a fine view of the dam and Lake Nasser. The lake extends over 500 kilometres south, past the Egyptian frontier and into the Sudan.

Industry of a different sort brought wealth to Aswan in pharaonic times. The beautiful red granite from which obelisks were cut is native to the town, and a few minutes' ride by taxi from the centre will bring you to the quarries. A mammoth

unfinished obelisk, fractured during cutting and abandoned, shows how these magnificent monuments were painstakingly hewn by hand and polished to a glassy smoothness.

Aswan is a good place to hire a felucca for a tour of the islands and the western bank of the Nile. **Elephantine Island,** the largest, holds the ruined Temple of Khnum, the work of many pharaohs down to the Ptolemies and even the Romans. The Aswan Museum, housed in a turn-of-the-century villa, is right next to the ruins. The set of stairs cut in the rock below the villa descends to Aswan's Nilometre, where you'll see the elegant marble water-level markers still in place. **Kitchener's Island** (or Island of Flowers) was a gift to the influential Consul-General of Great Britain in Egypt, and now serves as a botanical garden. It's one of Aswan's most pleasant places for a stroll. At the island's southern tip is a Duck Research Station—just follow the sound of the quacky cacophony. As you might imagine, this is a favourite destination for Aswan's children.

On the hills above the western bank of the Nile stands the **Mausoleum of the Aga Khan,** whose full title was Sultan Muhammad Shah Al-Huseini,

Aga Khan III, 48th Imam of the Shia Imami Ismailis, which is a Moslem sect whose adherents live chiefly in Iran and Pakistan. The Aga Khan (1877–1957) built a villa in Aswan just below the mausoleum, fell in love with the spot, and decided to stay forever. From the mausoleum, a path winds across the desert sand to the ruined 17th-century Monastery of Saint Simeon.

North along the Nile's west bank lies a typical Nubian village where life moves at an easy pace much as it has in centuries past. Ducks, donkeys and goats amble in the streets, young girls fetch buckets of water from a Nile canal, and groups of boys devote themselves to a hectic game of football. Remember that if you plan to photograph villagers, you must always ask their permission in advance.

Above the village, tombs of local potentates known as the Lords of Elephantine Island are carved in the rock. Some interesting traces of decoration survive, as do pigeons and bats in disconcerting abundance. A few tombs contain stone blocks on which offerings were sacrificed, and one tomb, the 12th Dynasty tomb of Sarambot I (or Sirenput), is complete with the mummy of Mrs. Sarambot who welcomes you in, "staring" with eyeless sockets in the shadowy light. With a few actors and a camera crew, these tombs would yield a very convincing horror film in no time at all. But they are among the oldest in Egypt, and a visit to the hillside ledge affords a fine view of Aswan and the Nile.

Aswan has its share of great pharaonic temples. When many were threatened by the rising waters of Lake Nasser during construction of the High Dam, the most important ones were moved to higher ground.

Take the short taxi ride from town to the dock for rental boats to **Philae.** The temples now on Philae Island stood partially submerged ever since construction of the first Aswan dam around 1900, but the operations of the High Dam threatened them with total disappearance. An international rescue effort was coordinated by UNESCO, and the temples are being reconstructed on another nearby island, very close to their original site.

The **Great Temple of Isis** flourished about the time of Christ, and is the largest and most distinctive of the island temples. Its great pylon has one of those useful secret stairways which photographers and acrophiles love, and the caretaker will take delight in pointing out where it begins.

Another taxi-ride to a different dock, and then a rental boat, will get you to **temples** from Kalabsha, which were once located on the banks of the Nile some 50 kilometres to the south. The temples were moved here closer to Aswan and to its appreciative tourists with the generous financial help of the Federal Republic of Germany. Largest is the **Temple of Mandoulis,** a classic Egyptian temple built in Roman times. To the left of the entrance to Mandoulis is the pretty little **Temple of Kertassi,** with capitals bearing the half-human, half-bovine face of Hathor. Behind the Temple of Mandoulis is **Beit El-Wali,** moved with American aid from its former site. The temple's murals show the military campaigns of Ramesis II in wars against various unattractive and easily defeated foreign enemies.

Abu Simbel

Of the many thrills which await visitors to Egypt, from that first glimpse of the pyramids to a quiet moment in Karnak's great hypostyle hall, few are more moving than when one stands face-to-face with the four colossal statues of Ramesis II at Abu Simbel. If possible, stay overnight at the small hotel here and rise early to see the sun illuminate the temple façade and penetrate to the depths of its inner sanctum.

Here at the limits of Upper Egypt, Ramesis II built his temple in honour of Harmakhis (Guardian of the Gates to the Nether World), Amon-Ra (Solar God), Ptah (God of Creativity), and in honour of himself, Ramesis II. The **four colossal figures,** 60 feet high and directly facing the rising sun, are all of pharaoh himself, with his queen and daughters at his feet. Above the entryway is the high-relief figure of Amon-Ra. A row of baboons, symbols of wisdom, sit hunched along the upper border of the tall façade. More tremendous statues surround you as you enter the **temple,** these being of Ramesis II in the guise of Osiris. Bas-reliefs on all sides tell of the monarch's generous offerings to the gods, of his triumphant military campaigns, and his merciless treatment of captives. In the very depths of the temple, Ramesis II sits in state with the gods to whom the construction is dedicated. The perfection of Ramesis' accomplishment is echoed in the restoration work engineered by a Swedish firm and carried out in 1968–72 by UNESCO. A doorway to the right of the façade leads to the interior of the artificial moun-

For prolific builder Ramesis II, happiness was reproduction—of himself.

tain made to receive the temple. Charts and diagrams tell the story (in English) of the temple's move from a spot now inundated by Lake Nasser to its new, air-conditioned man-made site.

The caretaker, bearing the giant *ankh* (life symbol) which is the temple key, will let you into the smaller **Temple of Hathor.** Four of the statues on the façade are of Ramesis II, while the other two show his queen, Nefertari, dressed as the goddess Hathor. Interior decoration is heavily in favour of the feminine side of the Egyptian pantheon although, predictably, Ramesis II is here as well. The benevolent cow in the depths of the temple is Hathor in her animal guise.

Photographers should visit Abu Simbel as early as possible, for the statues throw heavy shadows as the day wears on. Everyone who arrives at this spellbinding place, over 600 miles from the noise and bustle of Cairo, will want to take a few peaceful moments to gaze at Lake Nasser, a tranquil sea in the midst of the timeless desert. **83**

What to Do

Shopping

Cairo's **Khan el-Khalili** is world-famous for its wealth of things to buy. Antique or modern, simple or elegant, some handicraft item is bound to draw your eye. You'll need to haggle, but will be rewarded for your efforts by a truly remarkable change in price. Don't take a guide or interpreter when you go shopping as it is standard practice for him to get a kick-back on every purchase. Sometimes, a detour to the workshop in a back street or roof-top room will give you the chance to buy at a reduced price.

Here are some of Egypt's best buys, available in Khan El-Khalili and in tourist shops and markets in other cities, too:

Alabaster. The word itself is said to derive from the name of an Egyptian town. Shops sell statuettes, cigarette boxes, flower vases and similar items made from it. The stone comes from the Nile Valley and is worked, among other places, in Luxor.

Antiquities. Believe it or not, you can actually buy a piece of jewellery or an artefact from pharaonic times. Dealers who are licensed by the government to trade in antiquities display their licences prominently. You should only buy from one of these dealers. It's against the law to buy or sell true antiquities otherwise, and there are dozens of fake pieces on the market which, presumably, a licensed dealer wouldn't touch.

Copper and Brass. The tinkling of coppersmith's ham-

84

mers is a familiar sound in Khan el-Khalili. The best trays, Turkish coffee sets, samovars and other items are generally the older ones, but new copper and brass pieces are often cheaper, and still attractive and useful. It takes about a day and a half to chisel the arabesques into a small copper serving tray.

Cotton goods. Egyptian cotton's long fibres and smooth finish make it among the highest grades in the world. Mohammed Ali built the

Gimcracks, antiquities, beguiling folk-arts: the choice is yours.

women. Be sure to look at several sizes and qualities of cloth: unpolished cotton will be cheaper than the more chic polished cloth.

Jewellery. Gold and silver jewellery is often sold by weight with only a small mark-up for the exquisite detailed workmanship. Take your pick from pharaonic styles inspired by King Tutankhamon's treasure, arabesques, or modern pieces. Precious and semi-precious stones are also sold by weight at attractive prices, whether set in a piece of jewellery or not.

Leather Goods. Handbags, satchels and shoulder bags are all good buys if you bargain well, but it's important to inspect each piece very carefully for flaws and careless workmanship. Some shops sell camel saddles. They're hard to find outside of Egypt, but before buying you should ask yourself: does my camel really need a new one yet?

Tapestries. The eye-catching designs worked in cloth by the children of El-Harraniye (a village between Giza and Saqqara) can brighten any wall or liven any table-top. They come in different sizes, although colours and motifs will probably be your criteria of choice. The true Harraniye tapestries tend to be rather expensive, and

wealth of his dynasty on cotton. Many shirt-makers' shops throughout Egypt will stitch up shirts to your order in a few days' time, or you can choose from the ready-made ones. *Gallabiyas*, the long and loose Egyptian outergarments, are comfortable and attractive, and are made for both men and you may want to look at the less expensive copies and imitations (good and bad) which have come on the market.

Woodwork. Some of the most attractive woodwork in the world comes from Egypt. Foremost is *mousharabiyeh*, the intricate screens of lathe-turned wooden lattice which covered Egyptian windows in the old days, shielding women from the curious stares of strange men. Screens, room-dividers and tray-stands are

Left, careful work makes each piece a unique treasure. Below, cloth for sale in Khan El-Khalili.

sold at reasonable prices, but you ought to consider the problems of transportation before you buy. An alternative choice, easily jammed into a suitcase, is a small box of cedar or sandalwood inlaid with bits of ivory, mother-of-pearl and ebony. Each tiny piece of inlay is glued in by hand, set in place with a pair of tweezers. If you have space in your luggage, consider one of the larger boxes or perhaps an inlaid chessboard or small table.

Folklore and Festivals

Festival time in Egypt finds everyone outdoors, following processions in the streets, strolling along the Nile, or filling the parks and gardens. Vendors sell snacks and refreshing drinks, and the crowds eagerly pay court to itinerant performers. Wrestlers, dancers and singers all put on open-air shows, happily collecting coins at the end of the performance.

A favourite diversion is the

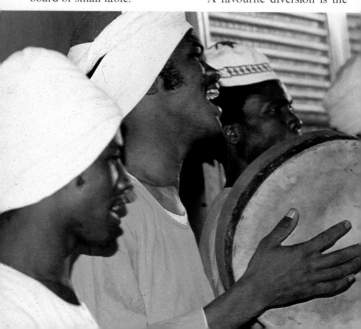

mock-battle called El-Tahtib: two men, armed with stout reed staffs, face each other and walk in a circle while swinging the staffs above their heads. It looks like a courtly dance, but each combatant is tingling with alertness, waiting for the opportunity to take a swing at his opponent. A split-second of inattention by one player, and the heavy staff of the other speeds down, but there's time to parry, and the two weapons meet with a resounding thwack. With equally-matched players. El-Tahtib becomes a graceful ceremony of smooth movements and mutual respect. But let a wily old master take on a young and inexperienced hot-blood, and the blows fall thick and fast. Strength and agility are less important than experience and alertness, and the old man

Lively African rhythms punctuate Nubian songs. In El-Tahtib, one inattentive moment spells defeat.

always ends up teaching the novice a few fine tricks.

In Upper Egypt, Nubian folklore and music is very different from the Arabic folklore of Cairo and the delta. Nubians have their own languages (though most speak Arabic as well), and traditional Nubian music sounds surprisingly Far Eastern in its tonalities and rhythms.

All Egyptians are united in the celebration of major Islamic and traditional festivals. The National Spring Festival, Sham en-Nessim, comes on the Monday following Coptic Easter. It's an excuse for everyone to get outdoors or into boats on the Nile in order to obey an old legend. "He who sniffs the first spring zephyr", so it goes, "will have good health all year". Another major holiday is Mulid en-Nabi, the Prophet's Birthday, when a mammoth procession winds through Cairo's streets, imitated by smaller ones in other cities.

Ramadan, the ninth month of the Moslem lunar calendar, is a holy month during which good Moslems fast between sunrise and sunset. Rules are strict: no food or drink, smoking, or even licking a stamp beginning at the hour "when the black and white hairs in a man's beard can be distinguished without aid of artificial light". But the fast is broken at sunset, and special dishes fill the feast tables for the early evening breakfast meal of *iftar*. Children, pregnant women, travellers and the infirm are exempted from the fast, and everyone else takes advantage of shorter working hours. Tourist hotels and restaurants keep normal, year-round hours for the convenience of non-Moslem visitors though many stop serving alcoholic drinks. At the end of the holy month comes Ramadan Bairam *(Eid el-Fitr)*, a three-day celebration marked by gifts of greeting-cards, sweets and visits among friends.

Perhaps the most sacred of Moslem festivals, Qurban Bairam *(Eid el-Adha)* comes in the middle of the month of Zu'l-Hegga, when many Moslems make the *hajj*, or pilgrimage, to Mecca. The four-day feast commemorates the biblical near-sacrifice by Abraham of his son, and Moslem families relive the moment by sacrificing a ram. After the ritual slaughter according to Koranic law, the meat is cooked and a feast is prepared for family and friends, with a generous portion going to the poor.

August used to be a time of elaborate festivals in Cairo. As the waters of the Nile rose in the annual flood, Nilometres all along the river would be checked and rechecked, and the readings sent off to Cairo by swift messenger. When the water level reached a certain high point, all the canals would be unblocked and the precious water would surge deep into the fields carrying valuable silt to replenish the soil. Now that the Aswan High Dam controls the Nile's flow at an even level all year round, the August festivities have only the faintest echo of their former gaiety and importance. Ignominiously, the festival might even be held in July.

International efforts to sponsor a new artistic and cultural Nile Festival in October are now bearing fruit. Luxor is the location, and concerts, art exhibits and folklore shows are on the programme.

Sports and Recreation

Cairo and Alexandria have many sporting clubs once patronized only by wealthy foreigners and Egyptian nobility. Today they're much more democratic, and tourists are invited to use the facilities as temporary or short-term members. In the heart of Cairo on the island of Gezira are dozens of tennis courts, a racetrack, an 18-hole golf course, squash and handball courts, several swimming pools and every other imaginable sports facility. A one-week membership is moderately priced. Make arrangements by calling the business office of the Gezira Sporting Club between 9 a.m. and 2 p.m., telephone 806000. Other clubs which take on temporary members are: Cairo Yacht Club, Heliopolis Sporting Club, Maadi Sporting Club, Maadi Yacht Club, Mena Golf Club and the Shooting Club.

Water Sports. As long as you don't swim in the Nile, you can enjoy a lot of water fun during your stay in Egypt. Besides the miles of beaches in Alexandria and along the Mediterranean coast, swimming opportunities are offered by almost every large hotel. If you're not a guest at the hotel, you may have to pay a small fee for the pool.

The new resort at Hurghada, on the Egyptian Red Sea coast offers hotel and beach facilities, and the best conditions in the country for scuba diving and snorkelling. Flights from Cairo and shared taxis from Luxor are the best way to reach Hurghada.

Riding. The most romantic images come to mind at the mention of a moonlight ride around the pyramids. But whether your preference is sunlight or moonlight, you can rent a mount for an hour or a day, with a guide or without. Rates are very reasonable, though you may have to do some haggling. Most exciting of all trails is the one which takes you from the stables at the pyramids of Giza along the edge of the desert to the pyramids at Saqqara and Dahshur. It's an all-day trip, exhilarating for an experienced rider, rewarding for an amateur, but probably too much for a person who is not used to being on horseback for several hours at a time. Make arrangements for your ride by going out to the stables right next to the pyramids.

Nightlife

Sound and Light Shows

The grandeur of the pyramids is magnified at night when powerful floodlights bathe the ancient stones with rich colour. A stirring commentary enhanced with symphonic music comes

from hidden loudspeakers. Sound and light shows at the pyramids are given in English on Monday, Wednesday and Saturday nights. Check performance times, usually 7.30 p.m. You can take a taxi to the pyramids and pay the entry fee yourself, or you can join an all-inclusive bus tour.

A similarly dramatic and informative show is held at the Great Temple of Amon at Karnak. After strolling through the temple, spectators sit in banks of seats behind the Sacred Lake.

Two important things to keep in mind for a sound and light show: first, no one ever seems to dress warmly enough, despite warnings of the evening's chill. In fact, the only times you're likely to get the shivers in Egypt will be when you look at mummies and when you sit outdoors to watch the sound and light show. Dress much more warmly than you think necessary. Secondly, take your camera and tripod but leave your flash attachment behind. Blinding flashes produce more discontented fellow-spectators than good photographs, as no flash has any effect at a distance.

Recreational possiblities are plentiful even in central Cairo. **93**

Cinemas

Look in the local English-language newspapers for current film showings. Something is always playing in English or at least with English subtitles. In Egypt's cinemas everyone has a reserved seat.

Buy your tickets an hour or more in advance (a particularly good idea on Thursday, Friday or Saturday night). Prices are very reasonable, and most cinemas are air-conditioned. Afternoon shows are usually preferable for those who want to hear the soundtrack, as at the well-attended evening performances, Egyptians have a tendency to chatter during the film.

Clubs

Clubs in the large hotels offer nightly variety shows, with Western song-and-dance reviews followed by fiery Egyptian music. When your blood is racing, on comes the belly-dancer, and the music builds to fever-pitch as she performs her sinuous gyrations and muscular impossibilities. Music for dancing follows. Though exciting and entertaining, hotel shows are not risqué, and can be enjoyed even by those who might take offence at the Folies Bergère.

Hotel clubs usually require that you have dinner. Cairo's discotheques and clubs called

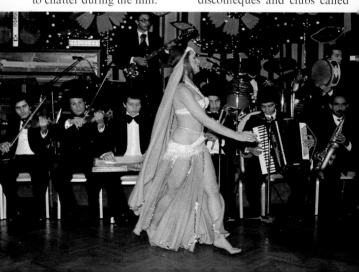

"stereos" have no such requirement, and are much less formal. Dance music is from the latest records, but a belly-dancer and oriental band often help to improve the evening's entertainment.

The Pyramids Road is lined with flashy nightspots, mostly for lone men with money to burn. It's generally better for couples to find the current "in" spot in the city centre.

Casinos

Foreigners are the only ones allowed into Egypt's gambling houses, so bring along your passport. Only foreign currency may be used at the tables. The Nile Hilton, the Sheraton and Shepheard's are the Cairo hotels with casinos. If you see "Casino" on a sign by a Nile-side nightclub, don't be fooled. Local usage of the word sometimes extends to dinner-and-show clubs which have nothing to do with gambling.

National Circus

Egypt's National Circus was started with the help of Soviet circusmasters over a decade ago. The clowns, acrobats and animals perform in Cairo's Agouza quarter during most of the year, moving to Alexandria for the hot months of July and August.

Dining

In a country with such a long history, it's intriguing to think that as a modern-day visitor to Egypt you might be eating the same as the pharaohs did. Certainly many things are unchanged. Mediterranean and Red Sea fish are served, and the Nile valley and the delta yield sheep, cattle, game, pigeons and ducks, grain and vegetables just as they appear in the old wall paintings. But more recent history has also had a culinary impact on Egyptian food. Italian, Turkish, French and English influences are all to be found in Egyptian cookery. Present-day internationalism provides an additional touch as well: from *chow mein* to *wienerschnitzel*, from Wimpy Bars to Colonel Sanders—it's all yours in Cairo.

Egyptians dine lightly at breakfast. In your hotel, the normal continental breakfast of coffee or tea, toast and rolls, butter and jam may be supplemented with salty white or pale yellow cheese, and fresh fruit juice.

Lunch is the main meal of the day, though many hotels cater to foreign habits and serve the big dinner in the evening. One o'clock until three or four in the afternoon is the usual lunch-break.

Dinner in Egyptian homes is traditionally served quite late, perhaps not until 10 p.m. or even later, though this is closing time for most hotel restaurants. During Ramadan all these hours, and many of the foods served, change completely.

Egyptian Cuisine

Your hotel is liable to serve more European dishes than Egyptian ones, but you should not miss any chance to savour the local fare whether at a simple snack bar or an elaborate Nile-side restaurant.

Start off with *molokhia* a green leafy vegetable cooked in broth with garlic, pepper and rice to make a hearty soup. Most Egyptians get along well on *fool*, a thick and savoury stew of beans flavoured with tomatoes and spices. It's delicious and is commonly served with oil and the juice of a lime or with *taamia*, a paste made of the same beans plus other vegetables, mixed with parsley and spices and deep-fried. *Bikli* (or *turshi*), spicy pickled vegetables, show up frequently on Egyptian tables.

Bread is the flat Middle Eastern type, especially well-suited for scooping up mouthfuls of *leben zabadi* (yogurt), or *tahina* (sesame seed puree), or its

variation *baba ganoug* (*tahina* with puree of baked aubergine/eggplant, lemon and garlic).

Some restaurants specialize in *kebab*, succulent chunks of lamb or mutton marinated in spices and grilled over charcoal on a spit. A variation is *kofta*, minced or ground lamb spiced and wrapped around a flat skewer to be grilled the same way, over charcoal, then served on a bed of fresh parsley or coriander leaf.

Fish from the Mediterranean or Lake Nasser is pan- or deep-fried, sometimes with an unexpected pinch of cumin added during cooking. Large Alexandrian shrimp are a delicacy, and are grilled on a skewer over a fragrant charcoal brazier.

Egyptians love to dine on pigeons, the birds being split and grilled or stuffed, served on a bed of rice. It's a rich-man's dish as there is not an abundance of meat, though the flavour is delicious.

Salads are served before and during the main course. Boiled cold beetroot is popular in season, and you will find it difficult to stop eating the excellent ripe sliced tomatoes and cucumbers with a dash of lemon juice or vinegar. Green salads may contain a tart, almost peppery green leaf called *gargir* mixed with the lettuce. Once you've tasted it, chances are you'll want to have it again.

Egyptian cheese is a disappointment, as even the best comes heavily salted. This may be good for water retention in a desert climate, but it's no treat for an unaccustomed palate. Processed cheese wrapped in foil is widely available.

For dessert, you can never go wrong with fresh fruits from the delta such as bananas, oranges, figs or guavas. A basket of dates will contain fresh dates, which are different to the dried, sweet dates you may have had elsewhere. Whenever you see it on the menu, order *ommu-'ali*, a baked dessert of rice, milk, raisins and coconut. It tastes delicious when made badly, and is heavenly when made well. Cakes and pastries are also easy to find, but must take second place to fresh fruit or *ommu-'ali*.

Tourist hotels often neglect to serve many delicious Egyptian desserts, but should you find

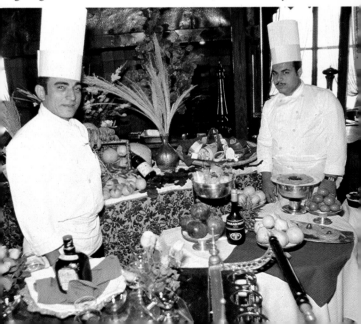

them offered, you must try *baklawa*, a many layered pastry stuffed with nuts and honey; an alternative is *'atayeef*, served principally during Ramadan, a deep-fried pastry with either sweet or cheese filling. *Mahallabiyah* is a fairly bland pudding of rice and milk garnished with nuts.

After the pyramids, what next? A peaceful Nile-side café or a cool drink in a shady bazaar—perfect!

European Cuisine

Traditionally in Egyptian tourist hotels, local cuisine is banished from the menu almost entirely and its place taken by "international" cuisine. Roast beef, broiled chicken and other hearty but undistinguished fare come accompanied by familiar soups and vegetables. The salads are the high point in such a meal. The very best hotels in Cairo and Alexandria may have foreign-born chefs who achieve good results in international

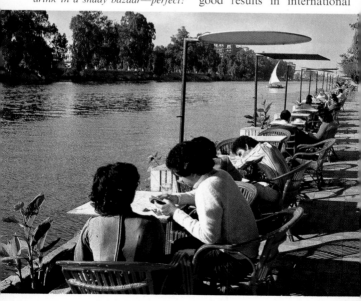

dishes and show an interest in local cuisine. But in most hotels and tourist restaurants the local chefs often lack enthusiasm for dishes which they themselves rarely taste. But don't leave Egypt with the impression that all Egyptian dining is unexciting: escape from your Cairo hotel one evening and search out a restaurant along Talaat Harb or Kasr El-Nil streets. With a little luck you won't be disappointed.

Beverages

Moslems are forbidden to drink alcohol. Though many Egyptians enjoy a glass of wine or beer, the religious prohibition of alcohol means that soft drinks are very popular, and found everywhere. *Sport Cola* is a very refreshing drink you'll be able to order. It is much less fizzy than you may be used to. Other cola drinks and fizzy lemonade are bottled locally, but you may also find them served in imported cans which, as a result, are exorbitantly expensive. Fruit juices and lemonade are almost always available and sometimes they will be fresh-squeezed. Be sure to try the Egyptian speciality called *karkadeh*, an infusion with a deep red colour and agreeable flavour, served slightly sweetened. It's delicious cold

at breakfast-time, but can be a bracing pick-me-up served hot as well. Hotels and restaurants in Upper Egypt, where the plant grows, serve it frequently. Sugar-cane juice is also cheap and flavoursome.

Egyptian vineyards in the delta have been cultivated for centuries. All hotel restaurants serve wine, though the selection may be limited, and service suspended on Moslem religious holidays. The price for a bottle of wine in a hotel restaurant will be about three times the shop price. Buy a bottle and have the steward mark it with your room number so that if you don't finish it at one meal you can enjoy it at the next. Of the reds, *Omar Khayyam* and *Chateau* (or *Kasr*) *Gianaclis* are soft, fairly dry, and have a good deal of tannin. *Pharaons* is less tasty and slightly more dry. White wines, not quite so good as the reds and invariably served too warm, are *Nefertiti*, *Cleopatra*, and *Gianaclis Villages*. If you prefer rosé, ask for *Rubis d'Egypte*.

Several imported brands of beer are served in better hotels and restaurants; always quite expensive. Local beer, a light lager called *Stella*, comes in enormous bottles which easily serve two people. It's quite drinkable, though *Stella Export*, in smaller bottles at a higher price, tends to be better. Quality is variable.

Local spirits are made from grapes or dates. *Zibib*, the Egyptian version of aniseed-flavoured *arak* (like *ouzo* or *pastis*), may be made from either grape brandy or date brandy. Many visitors find the grape variety preferable. Locally made vodka is good. Imported spirits such as whisky and cognac take prominent places on high-class hotel and restaurant bars. Prices are moderate to high.

Tea and Turkish Coffee

French or American-style coffee made in Egypt has an astounding lack of flavour, and tea *(shay)* is preferable at breakfast. As a refresher served in an Arabic coffeehouse, it will come with sprigs of mint. Stir a few into your glass: Egyptians swear it improves digestion and gives extra energy.

Turkish coffee is usually very good. It's served on the slightest pretext. An Egyptian host who didn't serve coffee to visitors—even on a five-minute visit to a shop, office or home—would be looked upon as a national disgrace. Most foreigners come to prefer Turkish coffee when it is brewed *mazbut* (with a middling amount of sugar). If it tastes too bitter order it *ziyada* (with lots of sugar). *Saadeh* is with no sugar at all. *Arrihah* means your tiny cup will come flavoured with just the slightest pinch of sugar. In practice, one is never quite sure exactly how the coffee will come, as one coffee-maker's *arrihah* is another's *mazbut*.

To Help You Order...

I would like a/an/some...   *orid*   اريد ...

beer	*bira*	بيرة	mineral water	*madaniyya*	مياه معدنية
bread	*esh*	عيش (خبز)	mustard	*mostarda*	مستردة (خردل)
butter	*zibda*	زبدة	olive oil	*zayt zayton*	زيت زيتون
cheese	*gibna*	جبنة	pepper	*filfil*	فلفل (بهار)
coffee	*ahwa*	قهوة	potatoes	*batatis*	بطاطس
eggs	*baed*	بيض	salad	*salata*	صلطة
fish	*samak*	سمك	salt	*malh*	ملح
fruit	*fakha*	فاكهة	soup	*shorba*	شوربة
fruit-juice	*aseer-fakha*	عصير فاكهة	sugar	*sokkar*	سكر
ice-cream	*glas*	جلاس (بوظة)	tea	*shay*	شاي
lemon	*laymon*	ليمون (حامض)	vegetables	*khodar*	خضار
meat	*lahm*	لحم	wine	*nibit*	نبيذ
milk	*laban haleab*	لبن حليب			

...and Read the Menu

فراخ (فراريخ)	*firakh*	chicken	زيتون	*zayton*	olives
حمام	*hamam*	pigeon	بصل	*basal*	onions
رنجة	*ringa*	herring	رز	*roz*	rice
سردين	*sardin*	sardines	طماطم (بندورة)	*tamatim*	tomatoes
بفتيك	*boftek*	beef steak			
ريش (كستليتة)	*riyash*	lamb	بلح	*balah*	dates
ضاني	*dani*	chops	تين	*teen*	figs
روسبيف	*rosbif*	roast beef	بطيخ	*battikh*	water-melon
كستلتة بتلو (عجل)	*kostaleta*	veal chops	فستق	*fostok*	pistachio
باذنجان	*bitingan*	aubergine (eggplant)	كيك	*kek*	cake
			مكرونة شريط	*makarona shirit*	noodles
حمص	*hommos*	chick-peas			
ثوم	*toam*	garlic	ملوق	*maslook*	boiled
عدس	*ads*	lentils	مقلي	*malli*	fried
بامية	*bamia*	okra	مشوي	*mashwi*	grilled

101

How to Get There

From the United Kingdom

BY AIR: First class, economy and excursion fares are available on daily scheduled flights from London's Heathrow and Gatwick airports. Irish and provincial flights make the connection in London for the 6-hour non-stop flight to Cairo. There are reductions of 50% for children between 2 and 12 years old.

Charter Flights and Package Tours

There are not many charter flights to Egypt. Those that exist usually form part of a complete—and fairly expensive—package, including accommodation and meals, tours to sites and reserved cabins on the Nile cruise boats. It is not possible to find a "flight only" ticket, or even a flight and minimal accommodation package, but as conditions are constantly changing, check with your travel agent before you leave.

BY LAND AND SEA: You can take the train, or drive your car, to Marseilles, Genoa, Naples, Venice or Athens to catch the ship to Alexandria. Few of these ships are true car ferries (though most carry cars), so it's particularly important to check sailing schedules and prices with your travel agent before leaving home as well as booking your passage at least two weeks in advance.

Some Mediterranean cruise-ships also call at Alexandria giving passengers the opportunity for a quick trip to Cairo and the pyramids.

From North America

BY AIR: Cairo is linked with one American city, New York, by daily direct flights. But there are also more than 30 other major American cities, as well as Calgary, Vancouver, Montreal, Ottawa and Toronto in Canada, that are linked with Cairo via daily connecting flights.

Of the two special fares for the tourist, the least expensive, the APEX (Advance Purchase Excursion) fare, is valid for a period of 6 to 60 days. The fare must be booked and ticketed 21 days prior to departure, and any changes or cancellations are subject to a $50 penalty. The 6-to-120 day and the 21-to-120 day excursion fares do not require advance booking and the tickets are valid for one year. In addition, a youth fare is offered for those between the ages of 12 and 23.

Charter Flights and Package Tours

There are currently dozens of GITs (Group Inclusive Tours) available to Egypt for periods of 7 to 22 days with Cairo as the starting point. Tour features include round-trip air transportation, hotel accommodations, some or all meals, transfers and porterage, sightseeing, the services of an English-speaking guide, taxes, and all service charges. Optional features include a Nile river cruise, lasting from 4 to 8 days, or an air tour to Abu Simbel.

On certain charter flights available from New York to Cairo, you may be able (with the help of a travel agent) to get a flight at a price that is considerably lower than the normal airfare.

When to Go

October and November are the most comfortable months to visit Egypt. April and May are also cool and pleasant, but are more unpredictable. Mid-winter weather can be very nippy although the constant dryness of the air and almost total absence of rain (except in Alexandria and along the northern coast) give Egypt a perfectly healthy climate for the time of the year. The winter season is the most crowded with higher prices and heavily booked hotels.

As all the best hotels, Nile cruise boats, tour buses and trains are air-conditioned, a visit to Egypt in summer is possible if you plan your sightseeing for early or late in the day, and take precautions against excessive sun and dryness.

The chart below shows average monthly temperatures in Cairo and Alexandria:

		J	F	M	A	M	J	J	A	S	O	N	D
Cairo	C°	14	15	18	21	23	27	29	28	26	24	20	15
	F°	57	59	64	70	76	81	84	82	79	75	68	59
Alexandria	C°	14	15	16	19	22	24	26	27	25	23	20	16
	F°	57	59	61	66	72	75	79	81	77	76	68	61

Planning Your Budget

To give you an idea of what to expect, here's a list of average prices in Egyptian pounds (L.E.) and piastres (pt.). Bear in mind that inflation is high in Egypt and many basic prices are even further raised by widespread tipping.

Airport: *porter* 15 pt. per bag; *taxi* to centre of Cairo L.E. 2–5, by *Limousin Misr* L.E. 4–6; *departure tax* L.E. 3.

Boat services: *felucca* (per hour for the entire boat) L.E. 5–10 in Cairo, L.E. 1.75–3.50 in Aswan and Luxor. *Nile Bus* 2 pt.

Car hire: *Fiat 128* L.E. 6–7.50 a day, 6–7.5 pt. per km.; *Peugeot 504GL* L.E. 8–12 a day, 8–12 pt. per km.; *Mercedes 230/4* L.E. 12–17 a day, 12–17 pt. per km. 100 km. minimum per day on all cars. Chauffeur-driven car L.E. 20 for a 6-hour day, L.E. 5 extra for a guide.

Cigarettes: *Egyptian* filter brands 28–35 pt. for 20, *foreign* brands 50–70 pt.

Entertainment: *cinema* 30–60 pt., *discotheque* L.E. 1–2, *nightclub* (for dinner) L.E. 4.50–10.

Fuel and oil: *super* 11 pt. per litre, *normal* 8 pt., *oil* 30–55 pt.

Guides: L.E. 3–5 half-day, L.E. 6–8 full day (depending on language).

Hotels (double room with bath per night): *luxury class* L.E. 35–55, *first class* L.E. 10–20, *second class* L.E. 8–15, *third class* L.E. 5–10, *fourth class* L.E. 3–6. Add 12% service, 2% national tax and 5 to 10 pt. city tax. Breakfast L.E. 1–3 per day.

Meals and drinks: *Continental breakfast* L.E. 1–2, *lunch/dinner* (fairly good establishment) L.E. 4–6, *fool* and *taamia* in a traditional restaurant 20–25 pt., *bottled soft drinks* 10–25 pt., *coffee* 12–22 pt., *local beer* 65 pt.–L.E. 1.05, *imported beer* L.E. 1.75–2.50, *Egyptian wine* (bottle) L.E. 1–3, *cocktail* L.E. 1–3, *imported mineral water* 65–90 pt. per litre.

Nile Cruises: cruise of 4 to 7 nights L.E. 190–275 per person, double occupancy; all meals and excursions to archaeological sites included.

Taxis: with meters 12 pt. for first km., 1 pt. for every 200 metres thereafter, no surcharge at night; taxi tour to pyramids (Giza) L.E. 5–7.

Transport: *bus* (ordinary) Cairo–Alexandria L.E. 1.55, *Limousin Misr* with driver, fuel included, in Cairo one-half day L.E. 12, full day L.E. 18, *train* Cairo–Alexandria L.E. 1.75–3, to Luxor L.E. 4.16–8, to Aswan L.E. 5.05–10, *air flights* Cairo–Luxor L.E. 25, to Aswan L.E. 32, Aswan to Abu Simbel and return L.E. 28.

BLUEPRINT for a Perfect Trip

An A-Z Summary of Practical Information and Facts

Contents

A star (★) following an entry indicates that relevant prices are to be found on page 104.

Listed after some basic entries is the appropriate transcription of spoken Arabic, plus a number of phrases that should help you when seeking assistance.

The information in this section has been carefully checked prior to publication. However, changes are bound to occur and we should be pleased to hear from readers of any new developments.

A **AIRPORT★.** Cairo airport is being modernized and though the departure terminal is pleasant and well equipped with café, restaurant, bar, banks (see MONEY MATTERS) and duty-free and souvenir shops, the arrivals terminal still needs work. Have patience as you enter Egypt. If you have not yet changed money, you'll need to change a small amount for porter's tips and taxis. Visas are available for those who neglected to get them at home (see also ENTRY FORMALITIES AND CUSTOMS CONTROLS).

Customs inspections are usually perfunctory. You may be asked to open handbags and carry-on luggage by security officers. It's best to keep cameras out of sight, as photography is forbidden at airports.

For help with airport problems, contact the Government Tourism Information Desk in the arrivals terminal near the exit doors. They may be able to help you to find accommodation, though space is rarely available on short notice (see also HOTELS AND ACCOMMODATION).

Make sure to book return tickets when you make initial arrangements for your holiday in your home country. Be certain to follow the regulations for reconfirmation of on-going or return reservations once you reach Egypt—flights are never sufficient to carry traffic demand, and you want to be sure of a seat.

On the day of your departure, allow *plenty* of time—two hours or more—to fight through Cairo's frenetic traffic so you'll be at the airport in time. The ride takes about 30 minutes if there is no traffic at all (as in the middle of the night). For details on airport transport and internal air routes, see TRANSPORT. Be prepared to pay an Airport Departure Tax in Egyptian currency before boarding the plane.

Airports at Luxor, Aswan and Abu Simbel are simple but adequate, with transport to the centre provided by both taxis and airport buses.

Taxi!	**taks**
106 Where's the bus for…?	**fayn al otobís ili ráyih…**

BAKSHEESH. Tipping takes on a wider dimension in Egypt. Baksheesh, which once signified a foreigner's giving money to an Egyptian for no apparent reason, is virtually dead in its classical form, replaced by the custom of tipping for every service—no matter how small. Egyptians who have little contact with tourists rarely demand baksheesh, but those who work in tourist-related industries often depend on tips for their livelihood (which is helpful to bear in mind when the soliciting begins). In general, the larger the tip requested, the less urgent the need of the asker. You will have to obtain a large supply of coins and notes of 5, 10, 25 and 50 piastres to keep your trip running smoothly. See specific tipping recommendations on the inside back cover, and remember that a working man's dinner costs about 20 piastres.

BICYCLE HIRE (*igár bisiklét*). Bikes can be hired in Luxor on both sides of the Nile. Rates are low—if you bargain well—and the equipment is basic. Bicycling is a good way to see the various tombs and ruins of Luxor.

What's the charge per day?   **bekám fil yom**

BOAT SERVICES*. The romantic *feluccas* which ply the Nile waters are practical as well as picturesque. You can arrange to hire a boat and helmsman in any Nile town or village; many *felucca* owners are used to tourists and often anticipate just where you'll want to go. It's best to save your *felucca* cruise for Luxor or Aswan as rates in Cairo tend to be high; if you want to see Cairo by *felucca*, find others to share the cost with you. Check at the dock near the Hotel Méridien in Cairo or the yacht club in Maadi to make arrangements; in Luxor or Aswan, ask any boatman on the river (or, rather, they'll ask you), and be sure that the price, length of cruise and ports of call are well understood before you weigh anchor. The Tourism Office has an official boat-rental price list, which may or may not be honoured by your boatman; it can serve as a useful guide, however.

The Nile Bus motorized ferry plies between Old Cairo (south) and the Television Building in the north. The trip takes about 20–30 minutes and is well worth it.

One of the most exciting things to do in Egypt is to take an excursion of several days on a Nile cruise boat (see NILE CRUISES).

CAMPING (*to'kháyyim*). Though camping is in its infancy in Egypt, several established campsites do exist. You can camp on Mediterranean and Red Sea beaches, or in other open areas, with the permission of the local authorities. Two primitive but conveniently located camping places are:

Pyramids Tourist Camp, 416, Al-Ahram Street, Giza; tel. 852202; near the pyramids, chalets and tent sites with running water, electricity and telephone.

Nasser's Camp, Abukir Beach, Abukir, 26 kilometres east of Alexandria; luxury chalets and tent sites.

Can we camp here?   **múmkin na'kháyyim héna**

CAR HIRE*. Few tourists hire cars to see Egypt as it is usually less expensive and more comfortable to strike a bargain with a taxi driver or hire a chauffeur-driven car in the cities, and to travel between them by bus, shared taxi, train or air (see TRANSPORT).

Should you have special reasons for wanting a rental car, several local companies and one or two of the internationally known firms have offices in Cairo and representatives in other cities. Arrangements are: minimum age 25 years, with international driving licence; minimum deposit of US$ 100 or a valid credit card. The rates on page 104 include partial insurance, but not 10% service and tax.

CHILDREN. Many things to do in Egypt are fun for children. In Cairo, whisk to the top of the Cairo Tower for the panoramic view. On your way to the pyramids at Giza, detour to the Zoological Gardens just across the University (El-Gamaa) Bridge for a look at wildlife of Egypt and the Sudan. At the pyramids, older children will delight in a ride on a camel or horse, padding from one pyramid to the next.

In Luxor, horse-drawn carriages and Nile *feluccas* provide the means for adventure, while in Aswan these two are joined by other attractions: the botanical gardens on Kitchener's Island, the dramatic observatory-monument next to the High Dam, and the Philae Temples, which must be reached by boat.

Whether you plan to stay at a de luxe hotel with swimming pool or not, you can spend some time with the children at the poolside. Most hotels welcome visitors to use their pools for a small admission fee.

As to baby-sitters, your hotel room-boy or chambermaid will be glad to arrange for someone to stay with children; in luxury hotels the bell captain can provide someone. Rates vary, often depending on the bargain you strike with the sitter.

Can you get me a baby-sitter for   **múmkin tigíbli murabbía il-láyla**
tonight?

CIGARETTES, CIGARS, TOBACCO* *(sagáyir, sigár, tobákko).*
Familiar brands of internationally known cigarettes are readily available from kiosks and hotel news-stands. They cost about twice as much
as Egyptian cigarettes, but are still quite reasonably priced by European
standards. Cigars and pipe tobacco are found easily.

Shortages often exist in the supply of Egyptian-made cigarettes, and
you may have to pay a premium for them. *Cleopatra* and *Nefertiti* are
long filter brands, mild and flavourful; *Shahir* is a good quality
unfiltered smoke; *Port Said* is the mentholated one.

A packet of..., please.	**élbit... min fádlak**
filter-tipped	**bifómm filtar**
without filter	**bidún filtar**
matches	**kabrít**

CLOTHING. Egypt's climate demands the coolest possible cotton
clothing for a visit during the hot months from May to September, plus
a broad-brimmed sunhat and sunglasses for both men and women. In
Cairo and when visiting mosques, shorts (on either men or women) are
out; women should have modest, longish dresses with sleeves, and a
head-scarf, while men should wear trousers and a sports shirt.

A comfortable pair of sandals (as flat as possible) and a pair of flat
walking shoes should cover footwear requirements for sightseeing and
shopping any time of the year. Comfortable footwear is *essential* in
Egypt for both the sand and rough stone terrain of the archaeological
sites—as well as for the city centre where road-works are constantly in
progress.

As most of Egypt's tourist hotels are luxury or first-class, men will feel
more comfortable at dinner in a jacket-and-tie, though there is rarely a
strict dress regulation.

In winter (November to March) it can be quite warm during the day
but surprisingly chilly at night. A warm pullover or wrap and some light
woollens are advisable.

Remember that Egyptian cotton is the best in the world, and shirts,
gowns *(gallabiya)* and dresses are moderately priced—you needn't
overload yourself with cottons from home.

COMMUNICATIONS. Postal service in Egypt is unpredictable. Post-
cards are taken less seriously than letters, and may be delayed. Even
letters may take longer than anticipated. Allow plenty of time, or resort

to telephone, telegraph or telex services for important messages. Also, have your mail sent care of your hotel rather than poste restante.

Post boxes can be bewildering: green boxes which bear a motorcycle picture are for express (special delivery) mail; blue, with an airplane, for air mail; red, with a train, for ordinary mail. In major cities, "express", "ordinary mail" and "air mail" are printed in block capitals in English on post boxes.

Hours: Cairo's main post office in Ataba Square is open from 7 a.m. to 7 p.m. daily except Friday, though many sections close at 5 (poste restante) or 6 p.m. Other offices are open from 8.30 a.m. to 3 p.m. daily except Friday.

Telephone: Egypt's telephone system has difficulty handling the volume of calls. You must have great patience when using the telephone, and it's not a bad idea to plan visits in person rather than make telephone calls.

Public telephones—which are rare but most commonly found in cigarette shops—may only be normal desk sets with a coin box attached; they take piastre coins. If you make a local call from your hotel room, you may be charged several times the normal rate.

To avoid hotel surcharges, go to a telephone office to place your call. You may have to wait some time before you get through, depending upon traffic—sometimes up to 24 hours.

Telegrams can be sent from telephone offices as well, and in Cairo, telex service is available too. Major hotels in Egypt have telex service at standard rates for guests, surcharged rates for outside users.

Telegrams, dial 124
Operator, dial 10

COMPLAINTS. In hotels, restaurants or shops, speak to the manager or proprietor; calm, courteous explanations of your complaint go a long way towards a solution, and a gentle hint that you are ready to appeal to a higher authority will usually break a deadlock. Most reputable establishments want to please you, so matters can usually be resolved quietly.

Should you have bigger problems, the tourism authorities are sympathetic, though the official complaint apparatus is ponderous. The quickest response comes from the Tourist Police, whose job it is to serve you and who take their duties seriously. See TOURIST INFORMATION OFFICES and POLICE for details.

CONVERTER CHARTS. For fluid and distance me[...]
112–113. Egypt uses the metric system.

Temperature

°C [-30 -25 -20 -15 -10 -5 0 5 10 15 20]
°F [-20 -10 0 10 20 30 40 50 60 7...]

Length

cm [0 5 10 15 20 25 30]
inches [0 2 4 6 8 10 12]
metres [0 1 m 2 m]
ft./yd. [0 1 ft. 1 yd. 2 yd.]

Weight

grams [0 100 200 300 400 500 600 700 800 900 1 kg]
ounces [0 4 8 12 1 lb 20 24 28 2 lb.]

COURTESIES. Egyptians long ago discovered the secret that a smile makes everything—and everyone—more pleasant. Though tipping may be a constant factor to reckon with in your dealings with many Egyptians, the smile is almost always sincere, and unrelated to the business in hand. Always shake hands upon meeting someone—Egyptians will often salute informally with the right hand before and after the shake. Other courtesies include never photographing someone without first asking his or her permission, and being very discreet about blowing your nose—especially in restaurants.

Egypt is one of the few Moslem countries in which non-Moslems are welcome to visit mosques. Be modestly dressed for your visit, remove your shoes before entering—an attendant will show you where to put them. It's better not to go to a mosque at prayer times, or on Friday, the Moslem Sabbath. If a few people are praying when you visit, avoid walking directly in front of them, and be careful not to disturb the tranquility of the place: flash pictures are never in good taste in a mosque.

Though tipping is found everywhere in Egypt (see BAKSHEESH) and it is usual to tip a guide or *gardien* of a mosque, tomb or ruin, from time to time a tip will not readily be accepted. Offer again; some Egyptians refuse several times just to show they don't require it from you.

...nd **THEFT.** Though crime is low among Egyptians, petty
pickpocketing are as annoying as everywhere else. You should
...o trouble if you take the normal precautions: watch your wallet
...urse in crowded markets and on trains and buses, lock your luggage
...fore giving it over to railway or airline porters, and don't leave valu-
ables on open display in your hotel room. If you have been robbed, the
Tourist Police (see POLICE) will do all they can to recover your property.

D DRIVING IN EGYPT

To bring your car into Egypt you will need:
- International driving licence
- Car registration papers
- *Carnet de passage* (without which you will have to pay a large customs deposit, refundable upon taking the car out of Egypt)

With these documents, you may bring a car into Egypt without paying
tax or having to pass an Egyptian driver's test. You will have to purchase third-party liability insurance in Egypt.

Driving conditions: Egyptian driving regulations were developed during
the British tenure (though driving is on the right in Egypt), but many
local customs have crept into usage; and the press of traffic and battling
for parking spots makes it inadvisable for a tourist to drive in Cairo.
Outside the capital, roads between the major towns are serviceable, but
full of surprises such as slow-moving vehicles, broken roadbed, pedestrians and stray animals. For information on driving laws and help with
any automobile matter, you can contact:

Automobile Club of Egypt, 10, Sharia Kasr el-Nil, Cairo.

Touring Club of Egypt, 8, Sharia Kasr el-Nil, Cairo.

Fuel and oil: For prices see page 104.

Fluid measures

112

Distance

driving licence	**rókhsit alkiyáda**
insurance policy	**bolísit alta'mín**
Are we on the right road for...?	**húa da tarík li...**
Fill the tank, please.	**imláha il tank min fádlak**
normal/super	**ádi/súbar**
Check the oil/tires/battery, please.	**min fádlak shoof al zayt/al ágal/ al bataría**
I've had a breakdown.	**arabíyiti itattálit**
There's been an accident.	**fih hádsa**

ELECTRIC CURRENT. Most of Egypt has 220-volt, 50-cycle electric current. Exceptions are some parts of Heliopolis and Maadi (suburbs of Cairo), which have 110-volt current, although these areas are gradually changing to 220 volts. Sockets are the European type with two cylindrical prongs. Many hotels provide each room with a candle in case of power failure. Often, the current is not up to its full voltage strength.

| What's the voltage, 110 or 220? | **kam al volt, míyya wa áshara (110) aww mitén wa ishrín (220)** |

EMBASSIES and CONSULATES *(safára; konsolía)*

Australia:	Embassy, 1097, Corniche el-Nil, Garden City, Cairo; tel. 28190/28663.
Canada:	Embassy, 6, Mohamed Fahmy el-Sayed Street, Garden City, Cairo; tel. 23110.
Eire:	Embassy, 2, Maarouf Street, off Talaat Harb; tel. 971687.
United Kingdom:	Embassy, 2, Ahmed Ragheb Street, Garden City, Cairo; tel. 28050/8. Consulate, 3, Mena Street, Roushdy, Alexandria; tel. 47166.
U.S.A.	Embassy, 5, America el-Latineya Street, Garden City, Cairo; tel. 28219. Consulate, 110, Abdel Nasser Avenue, Alexandria; tel. 801911.

E **EMERGENCIES.** If your hotel receptionist or a Tourist Police officer is not at hand, you can telephone these numbers:

Police emergency	122
Ambulance	123

ENTRY FORMALITIES and CUSTOMS CONTROLS. Everyone entering Egypt must register with the Interior Ministry at the "Mugamaa" in Tahrir Square, Cairo, within seven days of arrival. This may be done by the hotel, tour agent or host or individually. But it *must* be done. Late registration may entail a fine of L.E. 20 and a big bureaucratic row.

Visitors to Egypt need a valid passport and either a transit visa for a stay not exceeding seven days or a tourist visa for a period of one month (renewable for six months). Both are available from Egyptian consulates abroad, or from passport authorities at the point of entry for those who didn't manage to get them at home. At the time you obtain a visa (whether in Egypt or abroad), you will be required to change the equivalent of £100 sterling into Egyptian currency for use in paying daily expenses in Egypt.

Visitors arriving from an infected country without an international vaccination against smallpox, cholera and yellow fever may be put into quarantine (check with your travel agent about current vaccination requirements).

The following items can be taken into Egypt duty-free and back into your own country:

Into:	Cigarettes		Cigars		Tobacco	Spirits		Wine
Egypt	400	or	50	or	250 g.	1 l.	or	1 l.
Australia	200	or	250 g. or		250 g.	1 l.	or	1 l.
Canada	200	and	50	and	2 lbs.	40 oz. and 40 oz.		
Eire	200	or	50	or	250 g.	1 l.	and	2 l.
N. Zealand	200	or	50	or	½ lb.	1 qt. and 1 qt.		
U.K.	200	or	50	or	250 g.	1 l.	and	2 l.
U.S.A.	200	and	100	and	*	1 qt.	or	1 qt.

114 * a reasonable quantity

Currency restrictions: You may take up to L. E. 20, plus the obligatory equivalent of £100 sterling (see above), into Egypt and L.E. 20 out of the country. Foreign currency may be brought into the country in any amount; tourists will be asked to list all money they have on an official form, called "Form D", which must be shown along with the banks' currency exchange receipts when any remaining currency is to be taken out upon departure.

GUIDES *(dalíl).* Only guides licensed by the Ministry of Tourism in Egypt are allowed into historical sites. You can arrange for a licensed guide through any hotel or travel agency, but it is good practice to specify in writing what you want and what you are willing to pay. Guides may or may not be very knowledgeable about antiquities, and may or may not be fully fluent in foreign languages.

We'd like an English-speaking guide.	**aízin dalíl bil lógha inglízi**
I need an English interpreter.	**aíz mutérgim inglízi**

HAIRDRESSERS' *(salón tagmíl).* It's wise to have an appointment if you plan to have your hair done on Friday or Saturday, when barbers' and hairdressers' are busiest. Shops in Egypt often have long hours, from 9 a.m. to 8 p.m., and the normal Monday closing is usually ignored by hotel shops, making it easy to have your hair done any day of the week.

   Prices in the luxury hotels are like those at home—expensive by Egyptian standards, average by European. Independent shops are very economical.

I want (a)…	**aíz…**
haircut	**áhla sháari** (men)
	a'oss sháari (women)
permanent wave	**birmanánt**
shampoo and blow-dry	**shambú wa seshwár**
shampoo and set	**shambú wa fórma**

HOTELS *(fóndok)* **and ACCOMMODATION*.** See also CAMPING, NILE CRUISES and YOUTH HOSTELS. Egypt is in the throes of a severe hotel room shortage due to the increased interest in the country and its past from tourists all over the world. New hotels are rising fast, but it will be some years before supply can meet demand. Group tour operators usually have priority in room allotment, and so it is a very good idea to go to Egypt with a group and to have the agent make all the arrangements. If you go on your own, make reservations far in advance, be sure they're confirmed, and then arrive in Egypt prepared to claim your room forcefully—reservations are sometimes ignored, no matter how iron-clad they may seem. The same goes for cruises on Nile boats—make reservations early, and preferably in conjunction with a group tour. Competition for rooms is most intense during the prime months of the winter season, from December to April inclusive, except for Alexandria which is busiest in the hot summer months and virtually deserted from November to April.

Though Egyptian cities often have a selection of hotels in various price-ranges, luxury and first-class hotels are usually the only ones which tourists find suitable, although in the current crisis even some of these are lax in their service and upkeep. Spartan, though clean and presentable hotels of lower ratings can occasionally be found.

Children from 1 to 6 are granted a 50% reduction, 30% from 7 to 12.

HOURS. See also COMMUNICATIONS and MONEY MATTERS.

Shops

Open 9.30 or 10 a.m. to 1 or 1.30 p.m. and 4.30 or 5 to 7.30 or 8.30 p.m.; a few close on Fridays, but most on Sundays. Some shops work morning to evening non-stop (generally those selling imported clothes and knick-knacks).

During the month of Ramadan: 9.30 a.m. to 3.30 p.m. and often from 8 to 10 p.m.

Museums (in Cairo). Most are open every day of the week.

Largest and most important ones: 9 a.m. to 4 p.m., with a break from 11.30 a.m. to 1 p.m. or 9 a.m. to 12 noon on Fridays.

Smaller museums: 9 a.m. to 1 p.m., till 11.30 a.m. on Fridays.

These are the winter hours; in summer, some Cairo museums close at 2.30 p.m.

LANGUAGE. Arabic is not only the predominant and official language of Egypt, but Egyptian Arabic is widely regarded as a "standard" for the Arabic-speaking world in which dozens of Arabic dialects are found. Staff in large hotels usually speak some English and French, and perhaps a little German and Italian. If you need the help of a man on the street, English or French is the language to try.

The Berlitz phrase book ARABIC FOR TRAVELLERS covers most situations you're likely to encounter in your travels in Egypt.

Good morning	**sabáhil khayr**
Good evening	**masá'il khayr**
Good-bye	**ma'assaláma**
Thank you	**shúkran/muttshékkir**
Do you speak English?	**bititkállim inglízi**

LAUNDRY and DRY-CLEANING

LAUNDRY and DRY-CLEANING *(ghaséel; tandéef bil bokhár)*. Your hotel can arrange for laundry and dry-cleaning service, usually in its own plant. The best way to ensure quick service is to tip the chambermaid or room boy who takes the clothes, and stress the urgency of the situation. You may be surprised at the speed with which your clothes are expertly cleaned and returned.

When will it be ready?	**ímta takún gáhiza**
I need it...	**aízha...**
today/tomorrow	**ennahárda/bókra**

LOST PROPERTY.

LOST PROPERTY. An appeal to the highest authority in a hotel or museum can help turn up lost or misplaced items. On the train, speak to the conductor, or the station-master when you alight. If you've left something in a taxi, the Tourist Police may be able to help, as records are kept of taxi movements between hotels, terminals and spots of touristic interest; for things left in "limousines" hired from Limousin Misr, contact the company (see TRANSPORT for details).

MEDICAL CARE.

MEDICAL CARE. See also EMERGENCIES and ENTRY FORMALITIES. Ask your insurance company before leaving home if medical treatment in Egypt is covered by your policy. You might also want to have your doctor give you something against intestinal upset, just in case. Certain simple remedies can kill whatever-it-is quickly and effectively and maybe save a holiday from being spoiled.

Several specific medical risks exist on a trip to Egypt. In the hot months sunburn, sunstroke and dehydration are a constant danger, and preventative measures should be taken seriously. Bring insect repellant for use against flies and mosquitoes. Or buy one of the spray repellants readily available in Egypt, both local and imported; local brands tend to have more effect on local insect life. Less available is the rub-on repellant which is a useful item to pack, especially for sleeping with the

M window open. Also the waters of the Nile are inhabited by a dangerous parasite called bilharzia, contracted by ingesting unpurified Nile water, or through bare feet or skin in the water or along its banks. Don't swim in the Nile and don't walk barefoot near it.

Chemists'/Druggists' *(agzakhána).* Look for a sign with a green crescent, and either a green cross or serpent within it, and you've found a shop that sells medicines. Many stay open long hours—even 24 hours a day. Though they may not have the exact medicine you want, they may have the same preparation made in Egypt and bearing a different (but usually similar) name. The Egyptian drug will be a great deal less expensive than the imported one. Here are some of Cairo's better pharmacies, that cater to both Egyptians' and visitors' needs:

Windsor, 5, Tahrir Square; tel. 28171.

Zarif, Talaat Harb Square; tel. 756347.

Isaaf, 26 July Street; tel. 40369 (open day and night).

Pharmacie Dr. el Hakim, Osiris building, Zahraa Street, Garden City; tel. 20403.

I need a doctor/dentist. **aíz doktór/doktór sanáan.**

MEETING PEOPLE. See also COURTESIES. Egyptians have a long history of formal and flowery hospitality, now reduced to a few simple but very pleasant ceremonies. Tea, coffee, or a soft drink will be offered as soon as you take a seat in an office, shop or home. A friendly formality will prevail until you become better acquainted.

By the way, it is not customary for a host in a shop or office to give his guest his undivided attention; if there is an interruption, he will deal with it and then resume conversation with you. This method allows you to stay as long as you like without feeling you are keeping your host from his duties.

MONEY MATTERS

Currency: The Egyptian *pound* (L.E.) is divided into 100 *piastres* (pt.). The piastre is divided into 10 *milliemes* (mmes.). You may see prices written several ways: L.E. 1.50, L.E. 1.500 or 150 pt.—which are all the same amount of money, one pound and a half.

Banknotes are found as 5, 10, 25 and 50 pt. and L.E. 1, 5, 10, 20 and 100. You'll be able to distinguish coins (which are imprinted with Egyptian numerals only) most easily by their size and metal, not by the inscriptions on them. However, even this can be slightly confusing as millieme and piastre pieces are similar, and several different types of coins are used for the same amount.

They come in the following denominations, metals and sizes:

5 milliemes	brass, small
5 milliemes	aluminium, slightly bigger
10 milliemes	brass, smallish
10 milliemes	aluminium, slightly bigger
5 piastres	nickel, big
10 piastres	nickel, bigger still

It's a good idea not to accept particularly ragged banknotes as you may have trouble getting others to accept them—except as tips. For currency restrictions, see ENTRY FORMALITIES AND CUSTOMS CONTROLS.

Banking hours: 9 a.m. to 12.30 p.m., Monday to Thursday and on Saturdays; on Sunday, hours are from 10 a.m. to 12 noon, but some banks close on Saturdays and Sundays. All banks are closed on Fridays. Banking desks in the lobbies of the larger hotels have special hours for the convenience of tourists.

Changing money: It is illegal to exchange foreign currency except at a bank or other authorized establishments, and it's also forbidden to pay for purchases in foreign currency. Americans can change money at their consulate in Cairo at an advantageous rate; this service is offered by some other embassies to their nationals as well. On board Nile cruise boats, the purser will appoint an hour or two each day during which time he will change money. Always take your passport when changing money or traveller's cheques, and save the bank receipt which notes the transaction—you'll need it to reconvert Egyptian money to foreign currency.

At Cairo airport, there are bank desks before passport control for those who arrive without a visa and therefore have to change the required amount of foreign currency before getting the visa. For those who arrive in possession of a visa there are several banks and exchange bureaus beyond passport control in the arrivals hall and also outside the arrivals exit. Banks are located before passport control in the departures hall.

In Alexandria there is a bank desk at the docks.

Credit Cards and Traveller's Cheques: Very few establishments outside of airlines and luxury hotels will honour your credit card. Traveller's cheques are readily accepted by banks.

N **NILE CRUISES*.** Some hotels operate luxury-class cruise boats on the Nile, and many group travel firms charter less luxurious but still very comfortable boats and sell space on them through local travel agents. Your travel agent will be able to give you full particulars about accommodation on the boats, prices and departure dates. Rooms aboard cruise boats are often even more in demand than land-based hotel rooms in Egypt, so you'd do well to make arrangements as far in advance as possible. The normal itinerary is to start from Cairo and travel to Aswan, stopping at the major temples and ruins along the way, or vice-versa, a trip of 14 days; or, to travel between Luxor and Aswan (or vice-versa), a trip of five or eight days, depending on the boat. No matter how many days you stay on board, a Nile cruise will provide vivid memories for a life-time, and shouldn't be missed.

P **PHOTOGRAPHY.** Egypt has very few cloudy days, lots of bright sun, and sand and limestone which reflect a glaring light, so plan accordingly. Remember that you'll want to photograph wall paintings in dusky or even unlit tombs and temples.

Virtually none of Egypt's important museums allows visitors to take photographs, and you will often be asked to leave your camera before entering a museum.

Be careful not to take pictures of bridges, public buildings, airports, or any other subject which could be conceived as "military".

Always ask permission before taking photos—it's not appreciated if you simply photograph point blank.

May I take a picture?   **múmkin ákhod súra**

POLICE *(bolís).* See also Emergencies. Cairo and Alexandria city policemen wear white uniforms in summer, black in winter. In the provinces you'll see officers in khaki. Tourist Police officers, some of whom know a foreign language, have normal police uniforms, with a rectangular badge of blue-enamel-on-brass above the left breast pocket with the word "Tourism" (but in Arabic). You can contact the Tourist Police through any official Tourist Information Office.

In Cairo, the Tourist Police Public Service telephone number is 126. Their headquarters is at 5, Adly Street; tel. 912644

Where's the nearest police   **fayn a'rab ism bolís**
120 station?

PUBLIC HOLIDAYS. Moslem religious holidays are also national holidays in Egypt. If a Moslem feast lasts more than a day, shops and offices will close on the first and last days, and open with shorter hours on the other days. During the Holy Month of Ramadan, when Moslems fast during daylight hours, shorter working hours apply almost everywhere. Coptic (Christian) holidays are not celebrated as national holidays, though Coptic-run shops and businesses may close. The Coptic calendar differs from the Gregorian one: Coptic Christmas, for instance, is always on January 7th.

Secular Holidays

January 1	New Year's Day
February 22	Unity Day
March 8	March 8th Revolution
first Monday after Coptic Easter	*Sham-en-Nessim* (National Spring Festival)
May 1	Labour Day
June 18	Republic (Evacuation) Day
July 23	Revolution Day
September 1	September Revolution Day
October 6	Armed Forces (October Victories) Day
October 24	Suez Day
December 23	Victory Day

Religious Holidays. The Islamic *(Hegira)* calendar is lunar, with Moslem religious holidays falling 10 or 11 days earlier each year compared to the standard Gregorian calendar.

In Islamic reckoning, a day starts at sundown. If you're told tomorrow's a religious holiday, expect the celebrations to begin at sundown today. Businesses will close early on the eve of a holiday, and those restaurants which stay open may not serve alcoholic beverages.

RADIO and TV *(rádyo; tilivísyon).* Cairo has one television station broadcasting on two channels, the First Programme on channel 5 and the Second Programme on channel 9. The Second Programme has daily news bulletins in English and in French.

Egypt's multilingual radio station broadcasts from 7 a. m. to midnight daily, and in the course of the day has news and feature programmes in English, French, Italian, German, Greek and Armenian. For the schedule, consult the Cairo daily newspapers, *The Egyptian Gazette, Le Journal d'Egypte* or *Le Progrès Egyptien.*

R **RELIGIOUS SERVICES.** Egypt is predominantly Moslem, but foreigners of other religions have been coming to Egypt for so long that Catholic and Protestant services are held in Cairo, Luxor and Aswan; in Cairo and Alexandria there are synagogues as well. For a complete listing of Sunday services, consult the Saturday issue of *The Egyptian Gazette*, called *The Egyptian Mail*.

T **TIME DIFFERENCES.** Egyptian time is one hour ahead of Central European Time, two hours ahead of G.M.T. It remains constant throughout the year. In winter, when you are most liable to be travelling in Egypt, the time difference looks like this:

New York	London	**Cairo**	Sydney	Auckland
5 a.m.	10 a.m.	**noon**	8 p.m.	10 p.m.

What time is it?   **sáa kam**

TOILETS *(twalét).* Public facilities are located in important museums and terminals, and you may use those in the larger hotels as well. If you use the facilities in a café or restaurant, it's usual to order a coffee or a bottled drink. The attendant will expect a small tip.

Toilets are usually marked with symbols of a man or a woman. Sometimes the attendant will direct you to use the "wrong" one, but he has his reasons—more often than not to do with failed plumbing—and will stand guard to prevent embarrassment.

Where are the toilets?   **fayn al twalét**

TOURIST INFORMATION OFFICES. The Egyptian Ministry of Tourism has Tourist Information Offices in the larger Egyptian cities, and in many foreign countries as well. They can provide you with brochures, maps and other information on Egypt.

Cairo: Ministry of Tourism, 5, Adly Street; tel. 923657. (Other offices at Cairo airport and at the Pyramids.)
Alexandria: Saad Zaghloul Square; tel. 807985/807611.
Luxor: Tourist Market, just south of Luxor Temple; tel. 2215.
Aswan: North of old part of town, just off Corniche; tel. 3297.

Egyptian Tourist Offices abroad:

United Kingdom: 62 A, Piccadilly, London W. 1.; tel. (01) 493-5282.
U.S.A.: 630 Fifth Avenue, New York, N.Y. 10020; tel. (212) 246-6960.
3001 Pacific Avenue, San Francisco, CA 94115; tel. (415) 346-9700.

TRANSPORT*. Transport in Cairo is overtaxed, to say the least. Buses are so crammed as to be impractical, and the intense traffic jams make even taxis less than speedy. For trips from the centre of Cairo to the Coptic sights of Old Cairo, you may try the suburban train from Bab el-Luq Station, though this can be quite crowded as well at times. Alternatively take the Nile Bus to the Old Cairo terminus (see BOAT SERVICES). A 5-minute walk takes you inland from the Nile bank to the Coptic quarter. The boat trip is certainly a pleasant way back to the city centre after a rather musty morning in the churches. Walking, guided bus tours, or hired car-and-driver are the best ways of getting around Cairo.

Taxis: Taxis in Cairo and Alexandria have meters, but drivers cannot always be persuaded to run them—giving as an excuse that the machine is out of order. You should know how to tell the driver your destination in Arabic as few know a foreign language (your hotel receptionist should be able to help you with this). Taxi ranks exist near the larger hotels and tourist attractions (and at the airport), but the normal procedure is to stop a taxi in the street. Note that near each rank a Tourist Police officer will be on duty, laboriously recording the number of each cab, its time of departure and its destination. It's comforting to know that if you have any trouble with a cab you boarded at a taxi rank, the authorities will be able to investigate the complaint. It's customary to tip cab drivers: have enough small banknotes so you can give him the amount of the fare and tip, as he will rarely admit to having change. Official fares for cabs are quite inexpensive.

In towns where taxis have no meters, an official table of rates is established by the authorities, but it is sometimes difficult to discover what the correct fare should be. Often it is best to strike a bargain with the driver until you can get a list of fares from the Tourist Office.

Shared Taxis: Every city and town in Egypt has shared taxis for intercity travel. Fares are fixed, cheap, and the cars move out once full. The majority are seven-seat Peugeots, the rest Mercedes. Fare-supervision is strict and very rarely will the driver ask for more. Tips are not expected. Generally they will not operate, on a lengthy run, after 8 p.m. Cairo, of

T course, has several ranks—one for Alexandria, one for the canal cities, etc. The ranks are found close to the main railway station or bus station for a particular destination as the taxis absorb all the surplus traffic. Fares are very slightly more than the bus fare, sometimes less than the train fare (air-conditioned). Drivers will always approach you first. A group of four in a great hurry, for example, could leave immediately by buying the three remaining seats.

Chauffeur Service: Limousin Misr, a branch of the government-owned Misr Travel Company, operates radio-equipped Mercedes-Benz cars as taxis, airport transfer and sightseeing cars. Fares are very high by Egyptian standards, but moderate by European ones, and prices are posted in the rear of each car. Limousin Misr offers the most comfortable and reliable car service in Cairo; overnight trips from Cairo can be arranged as well.

Limousin Misr, Misr Travel Tower, Cairo; tel. 831358/824359/827029/836383/835174.

Horse-cabs: The romantic horse-drawn carriages you'll see in Luxor and Aswan are governed by an official price list. Consult the list in the Tourism Office before you ride—you may have to haggle for a price in any case.

Trains: Day trains operate frequently between Cairo and Alexandria from Cairo Station. Overnight trains equipped with sleeping and restaurant cars, and with air-conditioning, ply the route Cairo–Minia–Assiut–Luxor–Aswan and vice-versa. First class on the train is comfortable, second class is acceptable; make reservations early to avoid the disappointment of finding all seats and berths taken.

Internal Air Routes: Egypt Air, sometimes called Misr Air in Egypt, operates modern and comfortable aircraft on flights between Cairo and Luxor and Aswan, with several flights a day depending on the season. A daily flight from Aswan to Abu Simbel allows tourists to visit the famous Temple of Ramesis for several hours, with the return to Aswan the same day; or you can reserve space on the next day's return flight and spend the night at the one small hotel in Abu Simbel (have your reservations made in advance). There is also a twice-weekly flight to Hurghada.

Airport Transfers: Normal taxis and also Limousin Misr cars operate between Cairo airport and hotels in the city centre. The scramble for cars is sometimes intense, and it is not a bad idea to ask to share a cab with someone else—in Egypt, it's an accepted practice. In Aswan and

Luxor, both taxis and buses operate between the airports and central airline offices.

Taxi!	**taks**
What's the fare to…?	**bekám li…**
Take me to…	**khódni li…**

WATER *(máyya)*. Egyptians have a saying that if a visitor drinks even a little water from the Nile, he will return to Egypt for sure. Tap water in Aswan, Luxor and Cairo comes from the Nile by way of a purification plant, and is safe to drink though not very tasty. Whatever you do, don't drink *directly* from the Nile.

Hotels and restaurants catering to tourists, and many shops in tourist-frequented areas, sell bottled mineral waters imported from Europe which, though somewhat expensive, are worth buying if you have a delicate digestion. It is perfectly acceptable to take the unfinished portion of a litre of mineral water along with you from a restaurant or hotel dining room.

I'd like some mineral water.	**aíz máyya ma'daníyya**
fizzy (carbonated)/still	**gazzíyya/áada**
Is this drinking water?	**di máyya lil shurb**

YOUTH HOSTELS *(bayt shabáb)*. Hostels in Egypt's main cities offer students and hostellers a place to stay for a very low price, though standards of comfort vary. The best hostels are often full, and so advance reservations by mail are advised. For full information contact:

The Egyptian Youth Hostel Association, 7, Doctor Abdel Hamid Said Street, Marrouf, Cairo; tel. 43799.

There are hostels located at:

Cairo: Al Manyal Youth Hostel, 135, Abdel Aziz al-Saud Street, Manyal; tel. 840729.
Kohinoor Youth Hostel, 8, Shukry Street (near the Pyramids), Giza; tel. 852480 (groups only, by advance arrangement).

Alexandria: El-Shatbi New Youth Hostel, 13, Port Said Street, Shatbi; tel. 75459

Luxor: El-Manshia Street; tel. 2139.

Aswan: Abtal El-Tahrir; tel. 2313.

Index

An asterisk (*) next to a page number indicates a map reference. For index to Practical Information, see page 105.